10.95

The Voyages of
CAPTAIN COOK

The Voyages of
CAPTAIN COOK

DOROTHY AND THOMAS HOOBLER

G. P. Putnam's Sons, New York

Library of Congress Cataloging in Publication Data
Hoobler, Dorothy.   The voyages of Captain Cook.
Bibliography: p.   Includes index.
1. Cook, James, 1728–1779—Juvenile literature.
2. Voyages around the world—Juvenile literature.
3. Explorers—Great Britain—Biography—Juvenile
literature.   I. Hoobler, Thomas.   II. Title.
G420.C73H66 1983 910'.92'4 [B] 83-3263
ISBN 0-399-20975-1

Contents

The Voyages of
CAPTAIN COOK

Foreword

BETWEEN 1768 AND 1779, the Englishman Captain James Cook led three around-the-world sea voyages that resulted in the first real understanding of the size and geography of the world. Cook completed, except for certain details and refinements, the process of European discovery that began with Christopher Columbus's discovery of America.

The major purpose of Cook's voyages was to find the great Southern Continent that many believed existed in the unexplored southern regions of the world. Such a continent had been imagined by geographers as early as the sixth century B.C. Classical geographers knew the world was round and had some concept of the enormous land mass of Europe, Asia, and North Africa. It was thought there had to be a roughly similar land mass in the southern hemisphere to balance the planet. James Cook was only the latest in a long line of explorers searching for this vast continent and the rich resources it might hold.

The location of this hypothetical continent shifted as geographical knowledge grew. It was first thought that it was connected to Africa and India. But with the voyage of Vasco da

9

Gama around Africa to India at the end of the fifteenth century, that theory fell apart. At nearly the same time, Europeans were discovering that the world itself was larger than previously thought.

Five years before da Gama rounded the Cape of Good Hope, Christopher Columbus, sailing west to open a sea route to the Indies, had discovered America. In 1513, Vasco Núñez de Balboa marched across the Isthmus of Panama and became the European discoverer of the Pacific. More than nine thousand miles long from the Bering Strait to the Antarctic, and more than ten thousand miles wide from Panama to the Philippines, this vast ocean covers an area greater than the whole land surface of the globe. Its full extent was not yet known when Cook sailed 255 years later. Geographers after Balboa confidently mapped the location of the Southern Continent in the South Pacific.

Others had seen the Pacific long before Balboa, including the peoples living on the western coast of America. But it had also not only been seen but explored by people coming from Asia. These people were the Austronesians, who—many scientists today believe—set out originally from southeast Asia. Traveling in outrigger canoes, whose balancing spars enabled them to weather winds, waves, and storms that overturned single-hulled boats, descendants of the Austronesians gradually populated the islands of the Pacific.

As long ago as a thousand years before Cook, these ancient sailors learned to navigate from the signs of the sea and the stars. Sometimes lost, sometimes exploring or fleeing hostile invaders, these people eventually came to nearly all the lonely islands of the vast Pacific. As they spread themselves farther among the islands, the Austronesian language changed. East of the Philippines, in the island groups today known as Caroline, Mariana, Marshall, and Gilbert, the language and people became Micronesian. South of there, in the Bismarck Archipelago, New Guinea, Solomon Islands, New Hebrides, and Fiji, the language and people were Melanesian. Farthest east, in Tonga, Samoa, the Cook, Line, and Society islands, and finally Hawaii, the language and people were Polynesian. Though the appearance of the people varied greatly, there remained similarities among the languages of all three major groups. Unknown to Europeans—as Europe was unknown to them— these people developed cultures that would be unsettled forever by the coming of Europeans. Among Cook's greatest achievements would be his record of these cultures, and his attempts to understand these people on their own terms.

Many Europeans had visited the peoples of the Pacific before Cook, seldom with peaceful results. Ferdinand Magellan led the first European expedition to cross the Pacific. A Portuguese sailing for the Spanish, he set out in 1519, reached the southern tip of the South American mainland, and entered the strait to the Pacific that bears his name. It took thirty-eight days for Magellan to complete the grueling, two-hundred-mile passage. The great winds that blow ceaselessly from west to east around the bottom of the world make this one of the most dangerous sea passages on earth.

Magellan saw the island south of the strait, and named it Tierra del Fuego (Land of Fire) because of the fires that the islanders burned on the rocky islands at night, eerie and spectral to the Spanish sailors. Later geographers ignored Magellan's conclusion that it was an island, and assumed that he had sighted the Southern Continent. Crossing the Pacific, Magellan discovered the islands of Rota, Guam, and the southern Marianas.

The greater part of his circumnavigation over, Magellan was killed in the Philippines after unwisely involving himself in a quarrel between two groups of native people. Cook later cited Magellan's death to his shipmates as an example of the results that could come from approaching the peoples of the

Pacific with hostility. With amazing bravery, Cook customarily was the first to come ashore—unarmed, to show his peaceful intentions.

When the Spanish established their first permanent settlement in the Philippine Islands in 1565, they linked this base with their American colonies by developing a trans-Pacific route from Manila to Acapulco. Because their route lay north of the main Polynesian island groups, they remained unaware of them. Their landfalls were mainly in the Micronesian groups—the Marshall, Caroline, and Mariana islands. Few of these were considered of sufficient worth for the Spanish to establish colonies there.

The myth of the Southern Continent took on a new aspect: stories of vast resources of gold there. In 1567, Álvaro de Mendaña set out from Callao, Peru, and discovered islands east of New Guinea. The Spanish named Mendaña's discovery after King Solomon, who was thought to have a source of fabulous treasure as yet undiscovered.

Later explorers, including Cook, puzzled over Mendaña's uncertain mapping of the location of the Solomon Islands. Mendaña had fairly well described the look of the harbors and coastlines, but the exact location of the islands would not be rediscovered by Europeans for nearly two centuries.

Bad maps were a common problem of Pacific exploration, and it was another achievement of Cook's that the maps he drew were extremely accurate. After him, ship captains could set forth with confidence that they knew the location of the places they were going. Before Cook set sail, navigators had instruments that could effectively tell them the latitude of a place (the distance north or south of the equator), but not the longitude (distance east or west of any other point). Seafarers normally sailed to the known latitude of a given place, then went east or west until they found it. Part of every seaman's "charts" were descriptions or drawings of a coastline to allow them to recognize a place. But such methods did not work well in attempting to return to small islands in such a vast ocean. Mendaña himself was the first to try to return to the Solomons. In 1595 he led an expedition to colonize the islands. He took with him a Portuguese pilot, Pedro Fernandes de Quirós. With some four hundred people, including women and children, Mendaña's four ships embarked on what was to become a ghastly voyage of death. He landed first at some islands he called the Marquesas. Sailing on, he made landfalls in the chains of islands known today as the Cook Islands and Tuvalu. He was still far to the east of the Solomons, but had no way of knowing that. The ships were running out of food and water, and the passengers began to fight over the remaining supplies. Some 250 miles short of his goal, Mendaña landed at the Santa Cruz Islands, where he died. Quirós managed to pilot two of the remaining ships and the remaining passengers back to the Philippines.

Quirós knew from Mendaña that the people of the Solomons were dark-skinned, as were the inhabitants of Santa Cruz. Yet the people of the Marquesas were light-skinned and otherwise different in appearance. He concluded that as "God had not created them there alone," they must have come from the undiscovered Southern Continent, which must lie nearby, since (he reasoned) their frail canoes could not have carried them very far. In his three great voyages, Cook was to find that the people of the Pacific could travel great distances in their seemingly fragile craft.

Quirós now obtained a royal commission to search for the Southern Continent. On this voyage his chief pilot was Luis Vaez de Torres. Setting out in 1605, they sailed south of Mendaña's track, but threat of a mutiny caused them to turn back at about 26°S. The crew could read the signs of the sea, and the great swelling currents convinced them that there was no land in that direction.

Quirós reached the Tuamotu Archipelago, the easternmost chain of Polynesian Islands, and crossed the Pacific to the New Hebrides, which he claimed for the King of Spain. He called them Austrialia del Espiritu Santo. His three ships became separated, and Quirós returned to Acapulco.

Meanwhile Torres, commanding one of the other ships, sailed northwest. He ran along the southern coast of New Guinea and passed through the Torres Strait, which divides New Guinea from Australia. Reaching the Philippines, he submitted his report on the discovery, but it was forgotten until 1761 when the British captured the Spanish files in the Philippines. On his first major voyage, Cook was to gamble the safety of his ship on the existence of the Torres Strait.

The first English circumnavigator, Sir Francis Drake, in 1577 followed Magellan's route around South America. Passing through the Strait of Magellan in sixteen days, he emerged only to be blown back to the southeast, below Cape Horn, "the uttermost cape of all these islands," where he saw clearly there was no great land mass. His discovery was ignored by mapmakers, who cherished the idea of a continent that stretched from South America clear across the Pacific.

In the seventeenth century the Dutch were the leaders in Pacific exploration. In 1605 or 1606 Willem Jansz sailed south past the Torres Strait without realizing what it was and came upon the western shore of the Cape York Peninsula, in what is today Australia. Jansz did not realize it was separate from New Guinea.

In the years that followed, Dutch sailors explored other parts of the Australian coast along the northwest and south. These voyages culminated in the expedition of Abel Tasman, who in 1642 set out from Batavia, the Dutch trading port in the East Indies, to determine the extent of the land that the Dutch now called New Holland. Tasman found the island off the southwest tip of Australia that is now known as Tasmania.

He called it Van Diemen's Land after the governor general of the Dutch East Indies, but failed to recognize it as an island. Tobias Furneaux, the commander of the second ship on Cook's second great voyage, was to make the same mistake. Tasman sailed across the sea that today bears his name and arrived at the south island of New Zealand. He called it Staten Landt, believing that it extended across the Pacific to the Staten Landt that his countrymen Jakob le Maire and Cornelis Schouten had discovered off the coast of South America.

Tasman traveled up the west side of New Zealand, missing the strait that divides the two islands, and continued on to the northeast, where he found some of the Tonga and Fiji islands. Tasman had determined that Australia was not part of the Southern Continent, having sailed across the sea that separates it from New Zealand. He failed to map the eastern coastline of Australia, something Cook would accomplish later with immense benefit to England.

The last great Dutch exploration in the Pacific was the voyage of Jacob Roggeveen in 1721–1722. He was looking for the "high, mountainous" land sighted by Captain Edward Davis in 1687, some 500 leagues (1,590 nautical miles, or 1,830 land miles) off the coast of Chile, and thought to be part of the Southern Continent. Instead Roggeveen discovered the isolated Easter Island, which Cook would be the next to visit. Roggeveen sailed farther south than any previous voyager and at 62°S he sighted icebergs, which he reasoned had been formed in great frozen rivers in the Southern Continent. Cook, who dared go much farther south, farther than any man before him, was to come to the same conclusion, though he proved there was no continent in the regions in which Roggeveen searched.

With the eighteenth century came supremacy of the British and French in Pacific exploration. Both nations were engaged in worldwide competition for colonies and trading rights, and the lure of the Southern Continent brought them to search the southern oceans all around the world. The Frenchman Lozier Bouvet in 1738–1739 traveled far south in the Atlantic to latitude 54°S, where he sighted what he thought was the tip of the fabled continent. He called it Cape Circumcision, and the attempt to rediscover it would cause Cook much trouble. It is in fact the most isolated piece of land on earth, now called Bouvet Island.

An Englishman, George Anson, circumnavigated the world in 1740–1744, after which he declared that an English base in the Falkland Islands in the South Atlantic would be the "key to the South Sea." Cook was to find a better base for his exploration, but Anson's other work was vitally important to Cook's successes. Anson was rewarded for his voyage by an appointment to the British Admiralty Board. In that post he instituted reforms in the Navy that would make it possible for a man like Cook to become recognized and promoted to command. Furthermore, the voyage of Anson was ravaged by the disease scurvy, leading to a search for a cure. James Lind in 1753 recognized lemons as a preventive for scurvy, but his recommendations were not immediately carried out. Cook would enforce standards of cleanliness and diet on his ships that would keep his crew free of the disease and thus make his years-long voyages possible.

In 1764, British commander John Byron ventured across the Pacific, but proved to be a timid explorer. He surveyed the Falklands and claimed them for Britain. One of Byron's orders was to sail along the western coast of North America to search for the Northwest Passage that supposedly led through North America from the Atlantic to the Pacific. Byron virtually ignored this order and instead sailed as rapidly as possible across the Pacific, sighting only a few scattered islands.

The Lords of the Admiralty selected Samuel Wallis to command a second voyage in Byron's ship, the *Dolphin*. Accompanied by the *Swallow* under Philip Carteret, Wallis was to seek "that land or islands of great extent, hitherto unvisited by any European power . . . in the Southern Hemisphere between Cape Horn and New Zeeland"—in other words, the Southern Continent.

After a difficult passage through the Strait of Magellan, the two ships were separated. Wallis sailed with the prevailing winds up the coast of South America until he could easily strike westward into the Pacific. He followed Byron's track except that he sailed west slightly south of the point where the more cautious Byron had turned and because of that landed on June 23, 1767, on the island of Tahiti.

Islander canoes sailed out to greet the strange ship that had appeared. To the English sailors, as to later visitors, Tahiti was a paradise of green hills and palm trees. In the minds of Europeans, Tahiti would never lose its place as the most idyllic of the South Sea islands. Wallis claimed the island for England, giving it the name King George's Island. His success in firmly establishing the location of the island would offer Cook a base in the Pacific. Cook would bring his ships here time and time again, establishing friendships among the people, and would restore the native name.

After a month in Tahiti, Wallis sailed on. Land to the south had been sighted, again awakening thought of a southern continent, but the commander was ill and sailed for home.

Meanwhile Carteret in the *Swallow* followed the South American coastline up to Juan Fernández Islands, where he found that the Spanish had established a base. He made his way slowly across the Pacific, replenishing the ship's supply of fresh water at the nearby Masafuera Island and sighting the isolated Pitcairn Island farther west. Pitcairn was to achieve fame as the refuge of the mutineers of the *Bounty*, commanded by the notorious Captain William Bligh, who would sail on Cook's third voyage.

Carteret sailed on through the Pacific, searching for the

fabled Solomon Islands of Mendaña. He sighted land, but concluded correctly that the sighting was the Santa Cruz Islands. He actually sailed within sight of the Solomons, but concluded they were too far west to be the islands Mendaña had described. Rediscovering the islands of New Britain and New Ireland, which had been thought to be one island by English adventurer William Dampier in the seventeenth century, he also sighted and named the Admiralty Islands north of New Guinea. Finally he reached the Philippines, where he stayed for seven months making repairs to his leaky ship.

On the voyage back to England Carteret met a French ship commanded by the French nobleman Louis Antoine de Bougainville. Through an amazing coincidence, Bougainville was completing his own circumnavigation, in which he had followed much the same line as Wallis and Carteret. He stopped at Tahiti shortly after Wallis had been there, calling the island New Cythera. Landing at a different spot than Wallis had, he had no knowledge of the previous visit and claimed the island for France. Then he sailed west through the Samoan group and the New Hebrides, where he identified the Austrialia del Espiritu Santo of Quirós. Curious about the location of New Holland, as the Dutch called Australia, he sailed west to within sight of its eastern coast. On sighting the Great Barrier Reef there, he turned north and passed through the Solomons to the same harbor in New Britain that Carteret had visited and then on to the Dutch East Indies.

Both Carteret and Bougainville arrived home after Cook had already set out on his first voyage to the Pacific. Cook was to make use of the reports of both their voyages on his own later sailings. In retrospect it can be seen that both France and Britain were close to solving the riddle of the Southern Continent and establishing an accurate map of the Pacific. That it was England that accomplished both these goals was due to the genius of Captain James Cook.

CHAPTER ONE

Who Was Cook?

READERS of the *London Gazette* for August 19, 1768, found an intriguing item:

SECRET VOYAGE

LIEUTENANT COOK AWAITS FAIR WINDS
SEARCH FOR UNKNOWN CONTINENT SOUTH OF THE EQUATOR

Endeavour under its Commander, Lt. James Cook, is awaiting fair winds to begin its long Voyage to the Pacific Ocean island of Tahiti to observe, for the Royal Society, the Transit of the planet Venus across the face of the Sun.

Indicating that government leaks were part of eighteenth century British journalism, the article mentioned that the *Gazette* had received "Certain information to the contrary" that the *Endeavour* was intended merely to make a trip to Tahiti. Supposedly Cook had received secret instructions from the Lords of the Admiralty, the commanding headquarters of the British Navy.

> We have reason to believe these Orders are for a Voyage of Discovery, and will carry *Endeavour* to lands far distant in the South Pacific, and even to that vast Continent which is said to be quite as big as Europe and Asia together, and which is now marked on the maps as Terra Australis Nondum Cognita.

Cook was not a familiar figure to Londoners, and the article described him as

> a tall, impressive man with an agreeable modesty. His conversation is lively and intelligent, and in spite of his air of austerity he is well-liked and respected by his men. He has been commended to the Admiralty as a genius, well qualified for great undertakings. . . . We are confident that all Englishmen will join with us in wishing Lt. Cook and his men Favorable Winds and Good Fortune.

This was exciting news. The unknown continent below the equator, if as immense as imagined, would be a great boon to Britain. The size of the continent and its imagined riches could bring large profits in trade. Geographer Alexander Dalrymple wrote of it: "The number of inhabitants of the Southern Continent is probably more than 50 million, [and it extends] from the eastern part discovered by Juan Fernandez to the western coast seen by Tasman." In other words, it was a continent covering the whole of the South Pacific.

Cook himself is one of the strangest characters in this story, and his sudden appearance as commander of an important voyage must have seemed strange to a Londoner reading the newspaper account of his forthcoming journey. Cook was promoted to lieutenant for the voyage, an unusual achievement for the time, considering Cook's background. The readers of the *Gazette* in 1768 must have wondered, Who was Cook? Why was he given command of this voyage?

James Cook was born October 27, 1728, in the little English village of Marton-in-Cleveland, fifteen miles from the small harbor town of Staithes, on the North Sea in Yorkshire. Cook's father was a farm laborer who had come south from Scotland looking for work. He found both work and a wife. James was the second child, followed by six other children, four of whom died young.

As a young boy, James learned reading and writing from the wife of a neighboring farmer, who taught him in return for his helping with the farm chores.

When James was seven or eight, his father took a job as "hind," or foreman, of a large farm some four miles from Marton, near the larger town of Ayton. The proprietor of the farm, Thomas Skottowe, noticed James's brightness and paid his tuition at the small school in Ayton. James proved to be a good student; the schoolmaster remarked that he was "good at his sums."

In 1745, at the age of seventeen, Cook went to work for William Sanderson, a grocer and haberdasher at the port of Staithes. At Staithes a new yearning overcame his restless spirit. Staithes was a fishing port, where the fishermen went to sea in small, flat-bottomed boats with a single rectangular sail.

These "cobles" were reminiscent of Viking ships that had brought the design to England around the year 800. They are still in use today, and very likely the young Mr. Cook made his first sea voyage in one of them.

Cook was always fortunate in having superiors who encouraged his talents. Sanderson was pleased with Cook's work in the store, but saw that the young man's heart was not in the humdrum indoor life of a shopkeeper. Eighteen months after Cook came to work for him, Sanderson took the young man to Whitby and introduced him to shipowner John Walker, to whom Cook was formally apprenticed as a "three-years servant."

Whitby was a thriving city of ten thousand and one of the centers of the coal trade. More than two hundred ships a year left it for trips to the Baltic and Irish seas and farther destinations. It also had a ship-building industry. The "cat-built" boats with flat bottoms that were built there were intended for the treacherous voyage down the rocky east coast of England, carrying coal mined in Newcastle that was the fuel of the burgeoning Industrial Revolution. The cats, which Cook would later use on his own great voyages, had a wide and stubby look; their construction was intended to accommodate the largest possible cargoes. They were not swift ships, but Cook was to find that they could sail safely through unmarked coasts with dangerous shoals and reefs.

The journey to London, the usual destination, was short. A single ship might make ten round trips a year. It was good experience for a young man who wished to make the sea his trade. On the east coast of England a sailor would encounter rocky coasts with hidden obstacles, uncharted sandbars, uncertain tides, frequent storms, and the ever-present danger of shipwreck. For those who learned their trade well, there was the chance to rise to command.

Cook was a quick learner and used his spare time to advance

himself. In the winter months, when voyages were fewer, the apprentice stayed at Walker's home. Cook made what was to be a lifelong friendship with the Walker family. His studies in their household may have included astronomy and the mathematics necessary for calculating a ship's latitude at sea.

Every young seaman's education included the "three L's"— lead, log, and latitude. "Lead" referred to the method of gauging the depth of waters ahead. Particularly on uncertain coasts, men were stationed on narrow platforms near the front of the ship, from which they threw a lead-weighted line as far ahead of the ship as they could. Counting a series of knots on the line as it played out until it hit bottom, the men immediately called out to the helmsman the depth of the water. In the "chains," as these platforms were called because the men or boys on them were chained to the rigging of the ship to keep them from falling overboard, a young apprentice with a sharp eye could learn the shape of a coast and the signs of the sea quickly. He *had* to learn quickly, or his ship might strike a rocky bottom and tear a hole in its hull.

"Log" referred to the method of determining the speed of the ship. In its simplest form, the log was a piece of wood attached to a line whose length was marked by a series of knots. The log was dropped over the stern of the ship into the water and allowed to play out for a given period of time, determined by a sandglass. A calculation of the distance the log had traveled in the time elapsed gave the speed of the ship. The speed of the ship over a given period of time supposedly gave the distance the ship had traveled, but many other factors, such as currents and the drag of the line as it lengthened, made this an uncertain measurement at best. That was why the locations of isolated places, such as the islands of the Pacific, were seldom accurately known.

Cook learned to measure "latitude," or the distance of the ship north or south of the equator or any other given point, by using navigator's tools such as the compass and backstaff. The backstaff was used to "sight" the angle of the sun's passage through the sky; mathematical equations then determined the latitude. Slight modifications to the backstaff produced a more modern instrument, the quadrant, but essentially the navigator's tools of Cook's time were much the same as they had been in the sixteenth century.

Cook increased his knowledge of seamanship by studying the construction and rigging of ships being built at Whitby. Walker had commissioned a ship under construction there, and Cook took some part in the final rigging and fitting out of the ship.

At twenty-one, Cook completed his apprenticeship with Walker and joined a crew bound for Norway. He was out on the open sea, away from the coast, for the first time. Cook next went to the Baltic, and then back to Walker's employ. By 1752, he was made master's mate aboard the ship *Friendship*. Cook's promotion was due to the greater knowledge of navigation and seamanship he had acquired. That was his singular characteristic: He kept on learning, gaining new experience and knowledge wherever he could find it.

While in London with one of Walker's ships, Cook would have seen larger vessels setting out for the long voyages across the Atlantic or to the fabled lands of India and China. In wharfside pubs he might have met some of the men or masters who sailed on them. Perhaps the glimpse of a larger world stimulated his imagination of his own possibilities. Something drove Cook onward—that spark that separates the genius from those who are content with less.

In early 1755, John Walker offered Cook command of the *Friendship*. Surprisingly, Cook declined the offer and enlisted in the Royal Navy as an able-bodied seaman. This was the crucial decision of Cook's career. Ambition and patriotism were probably the motives. War with France seemed near, and the

Royal Navy was increasing from a peacetime force of 16,000 to a war footing of 80,000 men. Many of these extra men would be "recruited" by press gangs, who snatched men from merchant ships into His Majesty's Service at will. To volunteer for the service, Cook's ambition would have to be attached to an almost incredible confidence. The highest Cook could hope to achieve in the navy was master of a ship, and able-bodied seaman was far below that. Yet he declined the chance to captain his own ship. That we know. The reasons *why*, as so often with Cook, remain his secret.

Compared to merchant ship service, the navy was regarded as far harder duty. The eminent Dr. Samuel Johnson, who entertained his companions in the coffee-houses of eighteenth-century London with his witty philosophizing, once remarked that no man would go to sea who could otherwise get himself into jail. "For being in a ship is being in a jail," Johnson said, "with the chance of being drowned." He might have added the dangers of cruel punishment, scurvy, bad food, low wages, and no choice over ship or destination or captain.

Cook was assigned to the *Eagle*, a 60-gun ship commanded by Captain Joseph Hamar. A month after Cook's arrival, Hamar advanced him to the post of master's mate. Cook began to keep a personal log—a practice he would continue through his last voyage to the Pacific.

Hamar does not seem to have been a particularly able captain. The *Eagle*'s mission was to cut off French ships headed for or from the French territories in North America. Hamar chased one ship, only to find it was Dutch. He encountered a storm and thought the *Eagle* had suffered damage. After the ship returned to England for repairs, the damage was found to be slight. Hamar was ordered back to sea. After he decided to put the ship in dry dock to clean and caulk the keel, he was replaced by Captain Hugh Palliser.

Palliser's arrival was a milestone in Cook's career. As Palliser rose higher in the navy, he was to become Cook's most important patron. Under Palliser, the *Eagle* took several French ships as "prizes of war." Palliser took chances and extended his ship and crew as far as he could. He wrote to the Admiralty begging for a better crew. He did not overlook Cook, putting him in command of a cutter (a small sailing vessel used for fast journeys, communication with larger ships, and pursuits like those made by a modern PT boat).

In Cook's journal of his first "command" there is a drawing of a part of the French coast. He was already experimenting with the techniques of discovery, recording the look of a place so that he would know it if he saw it again. The cutter's mission lasted only two weeks, and Cook returned to the *Eagle*.

On May 18, 1756, war was officially declared between France and England, and what is known as the Seven Years' War formally began. It was a worldwide war, fought not only in Europe but in the colonies of America and the Indies.

The *Eagle* and another ship captured two French vessels, and Cook was given command of one of them to take home to England. Palliser in the *Eagle* followed soon after, intending to put ashore his prisoners and sick. Scurvy struck even in the English Channel, and 27 of the crew of the *Eagle* died of the disease during May and June. In addition, 130 men were so ill they had to be sent ashore to a hospital. Palliser himself had to request leave for recuperation from a fever.

The *Eagle* made several more expeditions off the coast of France in the year that followed. Palliser received a commendation from the Lords of the Admiralty. Returning to England in 1758, he received a letter from a member of Parliament who, at the urging of John Walker of Whitby, asked for an officer's commission for master's mate James Cook. Palliser was not able to commission Cook, who had too few years' service to qualify for promotion to the lowest officer's rank, lieutenant. But Palliser suggested that Cook take the examination for master. He did so, and on June 30, 1757, was awarded master's rank.

A master was responsible for the navigation of the ship, for her upkeep, stores, masts, yards, sails, and rigging. Though highly paid as a professional seaman (his salary might exceed that of lieutenants), his place in the hierarchy of the ship was below that of the commissioned officers. The captain gave the master orders concerning the destination, purpose, and nature of the voyage. Though he could overrule his master, the captain ordinarily left the details of navigation to him. It was a respected position, but few masters went on to become officers. To accept a position as a junior officer would be a kind of comedown, and the type of men who qualified as masters could not expect to attain the higher officers' ranks.

The British blockade of the French coast was an important part of the strategy of the war. The British aim was to starve out the French outposts in Canada, chiefly the two great fortresses that commanded the St. Lawrence River—Louisburg, which was the key to the Gulf of St. Lawrence at the Atlantic entry to the St. Lawrence River; and Quebec, the stronghold of French power in Canada.

One British attempt to take Louisburg had failed when bad weather doomed the expedition. On February 22, 1758, a British fleet under the command of Admiral Edward Boscawen left England for a second attempt. One of the ships in Boscawen's fleet was the 64-gun *Pembroke* under Captain John Simcoe, with James Cook as master. A combined land and sea force cut off Louisburg from reinforcements and supply, and on July 26 the French governor surrendered.

A day after the surrender Cook was on shore, where he met a man named Samuel Holland. Holland was using a strange device attached to a tripod. He would set the tripod down, peer along the top of the instrument it supported, and then make notes in a small book. Cook approached him and asked what the device was. Holland explained that it was a surveyor's plane table, and that he was making a military survey map. Holland invited Cook to return the following day to learn how to use the device.

Cook mentioned the incident to Captain Simcoe, who also expressed an interest in Holland's work. Simcoe was ailing and unable to leave the ship, so he invited the surveyor to bring his instruments aboard. By the time Holland arrived, Simcoe had recruited two other sailors to learn surveying techniques.

Throughout the winter that followed, while the navy was preparing for the assault on Quebec, Cook was getting the equivalent of a college education. There was "no room for idlers" on Simcoe's ship, Holland remembered, and Cook thrived under Simcoe's tutelage, learning astronomy and higher mathematics such as trigonometry, which would enable him to steer a ship through unknown seas and chart unfamiliar coasts.

Holland and Cook began to compile a chart of the Gulf and River of St. Lawrence. A chart of Gaspé Bay, farther up the coast, was published in England the following year and credited to James Cook.

The winter was a harsh one. The crews at Louisburg were restless; some sickened and died. Cook's log shows minor offenses punished, a court-martial, a stabbing, drunkenness, theft. The usual punishment was flogging, usually a dozen strokes. Although this sounds cruel, Simcoe was a relatively lenient commander. Men could be sentenced to flogging "round the fleet," where the punishment over a period of many days might total five or six hundred lashes. This kind of discipline was thought necessary to keep the crews in order. The men had been collected from many sources—some were actually kidnapped, picked up drunk in a tavern or alley and waking up the next day to find themselves in His Majesty's Navy.

In the spring, the British military commanders decided to move up the St. Lawrence with a combined force on land and sea. Between the British fleet and Quebec were four hundred miles of river. Much of the route was dangerous sailing. The French themselves had no really good chart of the river; the route for their ships was marked by buoys that could be recognized by the French pilots. Now those navigation marks had been removed.

To make things worse, the port at Louisburg was choked with ice until April 21. The commander of the English fleet, Admiral Philip Durrell, was not able to leave until May 5, venturing out on that day with thirteen ships, among them the *Pembroke.*

It was Cook's first experience with ice at sea. Fog rising from the ice made visibility limited, and the ships kept in contact by firing their guns. It was an eerie scene, ships navigating blindly through the fog with the muffled sound of cannon coming unexpectedly through the mists. Cook would hear the sound again near the South Pole.

Simcoe died at sea on May 15. His illness had progressed rapidly through the long, cold winter. Cook's entry in his journal is typically impersonal: "at 6 buried the corpse of Captain John Simcoe and fired 20 guns, half a minute between each gun." The new commander of the *Pembroke* was Captain John Wheelock.

Admiral Durrell advanced slowly up the river. From captured prisoners he learned that a new danger threatened. A French captain, Louis Antoine de Bougainville, who would later precede Cook as an explorer of the Pacific, had slipped successfully past the British and up the river to bring reinforcements and provisions to Quebec.

Four ships, among them the *Pembroke*, were sent to reconnoiter the most dangerous part of the river. Cook and the masters of the other ships made a quick survey. Guided by Cook and the other masters, 154 British ships threaded their way up the St. Lawrence without the loss of a single vessel. By the morning of June 27, the fleet stood within sight of Quebec.

Soon a fierce storm hit and drove several of the British troop ships onto the shore. The French commander, Montcalm, seized the moment to release his fire ships, vessels that were set on fire and sent without crews to drift into the English fleet. English sailors went out in boats to turn aside the fire ships. Miraculously, the fleet escaped without damage.

Now came the task of landing armed men on the shore at a place from which they could advance on the fortress. The ships intended to take the men ashore were flat-bottomed cats. Was there anyone who could give advice on such ships? The British army commander wrote of his good fortune in finding such a man. "The master of the *Pembroke*," he wrote, "assures the admiral that a cat can go within less than 100 yards of the redoubt [fortification]." But the attempt was a failure because the shoreline was guarded by a barrier of boulders on which the ships foundered, too far away for the troops to get ashore.

The English tried again and successfully landed troops on September 13. Wolfe, the British army commander, surrounded Montcalm's French forces on the Plains of Abraham. The ensuing battle resulted in the deaths of both commanders and the surrender of Quebec on the eighteenth.

Almost immediately, Cook was sent to Lord Colville's flagship, the *Northumberland*, a 70-gun vessel carrying five hundred men. Under Colville's direction, Cook assisted in preparing a complete chart of the St. Lawrence River. It was later incorporated in the standard reference work, *The North American Pilot*, and kept in use for more than a century. Cook by now had proved himself a master chartmaker. He would remain at work making charts from 1759 until 1762, when the *Northumberland* sailed for England.

On returning to England, Colville made a prophetic report on Cook's ability: "I beg leave to inform their lordships, that from my experience of Mr. Cook's genius and capacity, I think him well qualified for the work he has performed, and for greater undertakings of the same kind."

Cook now knew he was assured of a career in the navy, and the pay of a master was sufficient for the raising of a family. Within six weeks of his arrival in England and departure from the *Northumberland*, he was married to Elizabeth Batts. The newly married couple took lodgings in Shadwell and lived there until the following April, when the navy sent Cook to Newfoundland.

Thomas Graves, British governor of Newfoundland, thought the rich fishing banks off the coast could be better exploited by a complete and accurate survey of the island and the smaller offshore islands. Graves had become acquainted with Cook when the *Northumberland* had been there earlier and had heard from both Colville and Palliser that Cook was a highly skilled man. He requested Cook for the job.

Cook was engaged in the task from 1763 until 1767. It was a monumental effort, because of the terrain, the harsh winters, the necessity for thousands of calculations aboard ship and on land—when land was not easily reached because of the rocky coast.

Each winter during the four years of the survey, Cook returned to England. When he arrived home after the first year, on November 29, 1763, he found that Elizabeth had borne him a son, also named James, seven weeks earlier.

Cook's old commander, Hugh Palliser, became the new governor of Newfoundland. At his urging the Admiralty gave Cook his first real command, that of the schooner *Grenville.*

Though he commanded the ship, he was still not promoted to officer's rank.

Cook's first command prefigured his later career. Many young officers who served under him would go on to greater things—his first mate for the next two and a half years, William Parker, would one day be an admiral. Even at this date, Cook was concerned about the diet of his crew. His journal frequently mentions the shipboard task of brewing spruce beer, thought to be a cure for scurvy.

There was some trouble with the crew, for which punishments are recorded: "confined to the deck for drunkenness and mutiny" did not indicate a full-scale rebellion, but probably a refusal to follow orders while drunk. For the same offense another sailor was punished "by running the gantlope." The man was tied inside a cask whose top had been cut away, and dragged through a double line of his shipmates, who lashed him with knotted ropes.

It was on this voyage that a powder horn exploded in Cook's hand. He bore the pain for hours while the ship's crew made for a nearby harbor where there was a surgeon. The accident left Cook with nothing more than a severe scar; fifteen years later, that scar would be identification for the remains of Cook's body.

On his return to England in the winter of 1764, Cook was greeted with the news of the birth of a second son, Nathaniel. Cook spent the winter with his family, then set out for Newfoundland again in late April 1765. This year he surveyed the small islands of St. Pierre and Miquelon, and part of the coast of Labrador.

A dangerous incident occurred that would repeat itself in a more serious fashion on a later voyage. The *Grenville* ran onto a rock and had to be lightened by removal of ballast and watercasks so that the high tide would float her free. The damage was slight and the hole repaired. But the process of freeing the

Grenville from the rock took an entire day while the ship was at the mercy of winds and currents that might at any moment carry her farther onto the rocks and destroy her.

The charts Cook made were intended for the Admiralty files. But he obtained permission to offer them to a private London chartmaker for publication. Merchant sailors had to choose among a variety of charts, some of very doubtful reliability. The Admiralty gave its seal of approval to none, and a captain setting to sea had to buy his own charts, keeping in mind the old adage: Let the buyer beware. The only key to the reliability of a chart was the identity of its maker. A man like Cook might acquire a reputation for accurate charts that would lead to greater sales, and profits for him.

Cook set sail for the New World again in April 1766. In late May he found himself sailing among "ice islands," or icebergs. The summer was marked by rain and fog, but on August 5, the weather suddenly cleared. Cook was aware from his astronomical tables that an eclipse of the sun would be visible in this latitude on that day. He prepared his telescope, quadrant, and other instruments and made a careful observation of the eclipse, noting time of day and duration.

Eclipses were among those natural phenomena of great interest to the Royal Society, a group of English scientists who collected information and sometimes promoted expeditions for the advancement of science. The exact times of celestial phenomena, observed in different places, were useful in determining more precise locations in longitude. Cook sent his calculations to John Bevis, a student of astronomy and a member of the Society.

Back in England for yet another winter, Cook worked on his charts. Another was accepted for publication. Meanwhile, Dr. Bevis was polishing Cook's paper on the eclipse of the sun for presentation before the Royal Society. The paper was not delivered till after Cook had departed for the 1767 survey, but it received the Society's approval. Dr. Bevis called Cook "a good mathematician, and very expert in his business." This was high praise when read to a group that included the leading scientists in England.

By the time he returned from Newfoundland in November 1767, Cook had established himself as a competent mapmaker, astronomer, surveyor, and captain capable of commanding a small ship. By themselves, none of these qualities was rare, but the combination of talents that Cook had acquired through study and self-improvement brought him under consideration for another type of voyage.

CHAPTER TWO

Endeavour, 1768-1771

I

THE TRANSIT OF VENUS—the planet's passage between the earth
and the sun—would occur in the summer of 1769. This astronomical phenomenon, if observed accurately, could provide
information about the precise distance between the earth and
the sun. England's great astronomer Edmund Halley had in
1716 urged the Royal Society to send observers to several
widely spaced vantage points when the transit occurred in
1769, since there would be no such phenomenon again until
1874.

The Royal Society used its influence to obtain the support of
the British navy. Expeditions would go to Hudson Bay and to
the North Cape of Britain. It seemed desirable to have another
group make observations from somewhere in the Pacific.

The geographer and proponent of the Southern Continent
Alexander Dalrymple volunteered to command the Pacific
voyage. Dalrymple had worked for the British East India Company as a young man and had found a Spanish account of the

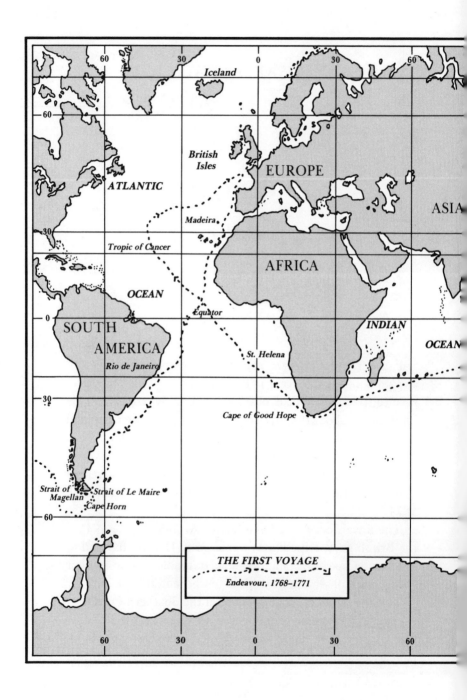

THE FIRST VOYAGE
Endeavour, 1768-1771

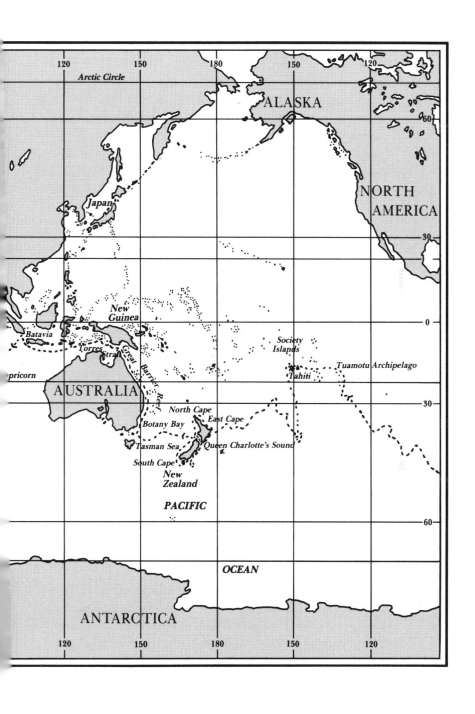

voyage of Torres and his discovery of the strait between New Guinea and Australia. Dalrymple was a knowledgeable man, but had devoted his career to attempting to prove that the scattered sightings of land in the south Pacific were evidence that a Southern Continent lay there.

The Royal Society recommended Dalrymple for command of the voyage to the Pacific. But the British Admiralty refused on the grounds that he was a civilian. Dalrymple was asked to compromise and serve as leader of the scientists under a naval commander. Dalrymple refused and Joseph Banks agreed to take charge of the scientific preparations for the voyage.

It was the opportunity of a lifetime for Banks. Though only twenty-five, he was the heir to a large fortune. Banks was typical of the educated European of his day in his interest in science. He had devoted his fortune to the cause of scientific discovery. He had already sailed to Newfoundland and Labrador in search of new plants, birds, and animals, and was a member of the Royal Society.

The reasons for the choice of Cook to command the ship were not recorded. The ship, already chosen, may have played a part in the decision: it was a cat-built vessel, of the same type as the Whitby coal ships on which Cook had learned the seafarer's trade. Built at Whitby shipyards, the *Endeavour* was a small vessel, only 106 feet long and less than 30 feet wide. Yet it was strong and had a large hold in which to carry supplies for at least a year's voyage.

Meanwhile, on May 20, Wallis and the *Dolphin* returned; the news of the discovery of Tahiti gave an ideal Pacific base for Cook's voyage. Several of Wallis's officers were assigned to the *Endeavour*; their experience would prove invaluable. Robert Molyneux was assigned to serve as master of the *Endeavour*. The master's mates were also veterans of the *Dolphin*: Richard Pickersgill, Charles Clerke, and Francis Wilkinson. John Gore, who had already been around the world twice, with Wallis and Byron, was named third lieutenant of the *Endeavour.*

Cook's rank was a ticklish problem at the Admiralty. The commander of a ship had to be an officer, but His Majesty's officers were generally sons of good family who had served in the navy from an early age to prepare them for the sea. A man without family connections who had enlisted as an ordinary seaman at a late age was not quite suitable officer material. Finally, Cook was appointed first lieutenant; though commander, he was not yet a captain. His second lieutenant was the twenty-nine-year-old Zachariah Hicks, an experienced seaman who, like Cook, had risen through the ranks.

The appointment of Cook as commander indicates that the position was not regarded as a plum to be given some ambitious, well-connected young officer. The Admiralty did not regard the voyage as an important one.

The presence of Banks changed the scope of the voyage. The rich young man saw this as the opportunity of a lifetime, and spent some ten thousand pounds of his own money to equip the ship with scientific equipment and hire talented scientists to go along. Among these were Daniel Carl Solander, a naturalist from Sweden who had been a favored pupil of Linnaeus, the famous botanist; his assistant, Herman Spöring; Sydney Parkinson, an artist trained to the techniques of recording precise details of botanical and biological specimens; and a second artist, Alexander Buchan.

One member of the Royal Society wrote,

> No people ever went to sea better fitted out for the purpose of natural history. . . . They have got a fine library of natural history; they have all sorts of machines for catching and preserving insects; all kinds of nets, trawls, drags, and hooks for coral fishing; they even have

a curious contrivance of a telescope, by which, put into
the water, you can see the bottom at a great depth, when
it is clear.

By May 18 repairs to the ship and rigging had been completed. There had been a strike in the shipyards and for part of
the time the *Endeavour* lay exposed to the sun in dry dock.
Some of the caulking work had dried during this time, and as a
result the *Endeavour* would prove to be prone to leaks.

Cook was unaware of the shoddy work that had been done
on his ship; he was busy supervising the provisioning. His attention to the health of his crew would be a distinguishing mark of
all three of his voyages. Wallis's men had remained remarkably
free of scurvy, apparently because of the experimental anti-
scorbutic foods that he took along. Cook asked for more of
these, and realized that frequent stops for fresh food of any
kind was a clue to the prevention of disease.

On July 30, Cook received his official instructions. The
"public" part of these was printed in such journals as the *London Gazette,* and it was well known that the purpose of the
voyage was to go to Tahiti to observe the transit of Venus.
Cook was instructed "to cultivate a friendship with the
natives," and for this purpose laid in a stock of beads, trinkets,
and other trade goods.

"But," the instructions continued, "as Captain Wallis has
represented the island to be very populous, and the
natives . . . to be rather treacherous than otherwise you are
to be cautious not to let yourself be surprised by them, but to
be constantly on guard against any accident."

The "secret" instructions mentioned by the *Gazette* were not
made public because they might require Cook to sail into
waters and land at places claimed by the Spanish or one of the
other countries with which England was competing for new
trading posts and colonies. After the astronomical observations

at Tahiti, Cook was to sail south to find the "continent or land of great extent" that had been reported by some of the men of the *Dolphin*. If Cook did not sight such land by the time he reached latitude 40°S, he was to turn westward, where it was expected he would find "the eastern side of the land discovered by Tasman and now called New Zealand."

Somewhere, it was hoped, Cook would find the Southern Continent, and, if so, he was to explore ashore for anything of value; carefully "observe the nature of the soil, and the products thereof; make note of 'beasts, fowls . . . and fishes' "; and "in case you find any mines, minerals, or valuable stones, you are to bring home specimens of each, as also such specimens of the seeds of the trees, fruits, and grains as you may be able to collect."

The instructions were thorough. If there were natives on the Southern Continent, Cook was to "cultivate a friendship and alliance with them." Above all, "with the consent of the natives," Cook was "to take possession of convenient situations in the country in the name of the King of Great Britain; or, if you find the country uninhabited, take possession . . . as first discoverers and possessors."

Cook reached Plymouth, where the *Endeavour* was moored, on August 14. Banks, with four servants, two dogs, and the scientists, soon joined him. His influence caused the Admiralty to assign twelve marines and fifteen additional seamen to the voyage. There was some grumbling among the crew and junior officers, whose quarters shrank as room had to be found for the additional passengers. Cook set an example by sharing the "great cabin" in the stern (traditionally reserved for the captain) with Banks and Solander. There, he would continue his education by participating in the scientists' discussion of what they had seen and discovered and the implications for science. Banks and Solander had had the best educations Europe could provide; they now had a pupil whose mind absorbed knowledge like a sponge and whose own discoveries and observations would within a few years fill huge gaps in humanity's knowledge of itself and the world.

On August 26, 1768, with ninety-four persons on board, the *Endeavour* set sail. Those who survived the trip would not see England again for nearly three years.

Cook sailed south to catch the trade winds that would bear the ship across the Atlantic. Storms soon revealed the flaws in the ship's hull, but "worst of all," to Cook, three or four dozen of the ship's poultry were swept overboard. The ship put in at the island of Madeira off the northwest coast of Africa on September 13. The wine there was of good quality, and casks of it were taken aboard for the crew's daily rations. Cook also purchased an unusual addition to the ship's fare: thirty pounds of onions for *each* man aboard. Onions kept for a long time and served the need for fresh vegetables.

After the crew recaulked the ship's sides at Madeira, the *Endeavour* began the Atlantic crossing. It was a short voyage with good weather. The crew were issued pipes, tobacco, and hook and line for catching fresh fish. Cook kept the men busy on the principle that they were happiest when kept from boredom. The tasks he assigned them show the value he placed on cleanliness in keeping the ship free from disease. Both the decks and the areas between decks were frequently scraped and cleaned. Almost as often, the below-deck area was "smoked" with slow-burning charcoal fires and aired. This went against all tradition to the British sailor, who believed the dank, stale air below decks was healthier than the sea-breeze above. Baths were thought to be hazardous to health and seamen's quarters ordinarily stank with the smell of bodies, grog, and tobacco.

More than the enforced cleanliness, the crew resented Cook's dietary regulations. He might make them eat boiled "pease" (dried split peas) mixed with oatmeal or "portable broth" (a kind of bouillon cube), but they preferred familiar salt pork and hard, dry biscuit. Cook first administered twelve lashes to men who refused to eat fresh meat, but then tried a subtler method.

One of the experimental foods was sauerkraut, or pickled cabbage. Not one of the men would touch it. Cook gave orders that the sauerkraut should be served every day at the officers' table only. After a week or so of watching the officers gobble sauerkraut, the men then demanded their share. Eventually Cook had to ration it. "Such," he wrote in his journal, "are the tempers and dispositions of seamen in general . . . [that] the moment they see their superiors set a value upon it, it becomes the finest stuff in the world."

On October 25, the *Endeavour* crossed the equator, or as English sailors called it, "the Line." It was the occasion for a time-honored ceremony. A sailor was dressed to resemble King Neptune, the ruler of the ocean. All aboard ship who had never crossed the Line were brought before him and given the choice of paying a fine of a bottle of rum, or being ducked in the ocean. Cook was making his first crossing and chose to pay his fine in rum. The good-natured Banks paid in brandy not only for himself but for his four servants and two dogs as well. Twenty-two men chose the penalty, rather than give up what was four days' ration of rum. A rope chair was attached to the main yard (the crossbar on the main mast) by means of a rope and pulley, and each man took his dunking. The ceremony was conducted in good humor; Molyneux, the master, noted that the men "behaved with great spirit and gave universal satisfaction. The evening was spent merrily without debauch."

The *Endeavour*'s lookout sighted the coast of Brazil on November 8, and the ship made for the Portuguese port of Rio de Janeiro. The livestock aboard needed fresh fodder that was available here. Cook received a rude shock when the officers he sent ashore to pay respects to the viceroy of the port were detained by Portuguese troops. Soon after, Portuguese officers came on board and questioned Cook closely about the ship, cargo, and number of guns. Cook's officers were returned with the warning that no one but the captain would be allowed ashore.

Cook went to see the viceroy. He showed the Portuguese the letter from the British Admiralty certifying the official nature of the *Endeavour*'s voyage. The viceroy shrugged. Such things could be forgeries. The official's questions showed that it was the *Endeavour* itself that aroused suspicion. This small, flat-bottomed, clumsy boat was surely not meant for a voyage to the Pacific—it was meant for following coasts, for ducking into small harbors to escape a full-rigged man-of-war—meant, in short, for piracy and smuggling.

Cook held his temper. He explained the purpose of the ship in observing the transit of Venus. It sounded like a fantasy to the viceroy. He told Cook that if he found the regulations of the port too harsh, he might leave when he pleased. Cook finally obtained permission for a few men to come ashore to gather supplies.

The crew, anxious for shore leave, chafed under the restrictions. Cook had to order twelve lashes for a number of them caught trying to sneak ashore. He could not use the same measures to keep the civilians in line, and the impetuous Banks jeopardized his own, and the expedition's, safety by landing in a small boat in the middle of the night to collect specimens of the local plants. He bribed some of the Portuguese guarding the ship to bring him more plants. This activity aroused more suspicion, for the Portuguese thought it impossible that the "gentleman" would come so far merely to collect plants.

Cook was glad to see the last of Rio, as the ship departed on December 7 and made its way south along the coast. For all practical purposes, the men aboard were now cut off from the world they knew. If anything happened to the ship, only gradually would their friends and relatives in England come to the conclusion that they were never coming back.

Well into the Southern Hemisphere by now, where the seasons were the reverse of those in the northern half of the globe, the ship was in midsummer conditions. On December 30, swarms of butterflies, moths, beetles, and other insects flew about the sails. Banks gave out bottles of rum to seamen who captured specimens for his collection.

Conditions changed rapidly, however, as the ship sailed into regions that even in summer were never warm. On January 6, the crew sighted their first penguins. It was a signal to Cook, for on the same day he issued the men "fearnought" jackets and trousers made of heavy wool as protection from the encroaching cold.

On January 11, the ship came in sight of the large island of Tierra del Fuego, at the southern tip of South America. Cook now faced the treacherous task of "doubling" the Horn. Below Cape Horn, the extreme southern tip of the continent, winds unchecked by any land mass blow ferociously from west to east, driving back any ship that seeks to ride against them. Many times it took ships months to accomplish the task of fighting westward from the Horn and then north into calmer seas where the journey across the Pacific could begin.

Dalrymple, and many other geographers, felt that the Southern Continent could be found by sailing due west from Cape Horn. Cook soon saw the impossibility of this, though he made his way farther west in a "higher" (toward the South Pole) latitude than any commander before him. By the time he was planning a second voyage, he had realized that to explore the area west of the Horn, a ship must ride with the winds and tides and cross the Pacific from the other direction.

For now there were other problems. On the map, the Strait of Magellan appears to be the shortest passage through to the Pacific. Yet Wallis had spent three months in this short stretch of water, fighting for every inch of headway. Cook chose the Strait of Le Maire, which would lead the ship right under Cape Horn itself.

Cook realized that he must find an anchorage in the strait where he could put the ship in to await one of the infrequent favorable winds. On January 15, he found such a place, which he called Bay of Success. He went ashore with Banks and Solander and found thirty to forty people gathered along the beach. They were unafraid of the strange ship; three of them, at Cook's invitation, even came aboard for a short visit.

The Tierra del Fuegans, Cook wrote, were "something above the middle size; of a dark copper color with long black hair. They paint their bodies in streaks, mostly red and black. Their clothing consists wholly of a guanaco's skin or that of a seal, in the same form as it came from the animal's back." Their huts were fragile structures made of sticks with branches or grass for covering. Their light shelter and casual clothing, in this region of cold rain, snow, and hail, made Cook call them a very hardy race.

Even so they had no "government" that Cook could see, and had no "industry," because they had no tools, and for these faults he judged them "perhaps as miserable a set of people as are this day upon earth." Experience would in time lead Cook to a better understanding of native peoples, judging them by their own values, rather than those of Enlightenment Europe.

The *Endeavour* left the Bay of Success on the twenty-first of January, and fought its way to Cape Horn by the twenty-fifth. Cook's remarkable luck with wind and current, and his own navigational skill, brought him round the Horn on the following day. The "doubling" would not be complete until February 13, when the ship was finally free of the influence of the storms and tides that could actually carry a ship back round the Horn or dash it against the lee shore of South America. Nonetheless, Cook's doubling took only thirty-three days, a remarkably short time. He was now in the Pacific, the map of which was sketchy at best and wild guesswork for most of its area. By the time his voyages were complete, he would have mapped most of the vast Pacific with an accuracy that no one before him had even approached.

The only well-established point in the Pacific was Tahiti. By the beginning of April, the *Endeavour* was entering the thousand-mile long chain of islands called the Tuamotu Archipelago, just east of the Society Islands, where Tahiti lies. On April 4, the crew saw land for the first time since January 28. By the thirteenth, the ship was anchored in Royal Bay, where the *Dolphin* had been. It was a place that Cook revisited many times; he called it by the native name, Matavai Bay.

II

BETWEEN WALLIS'S VOYAGE and Cook's arrival, another European had visited Tahiti. He was Louis Antoine de Bougainville, whose tale of an island paradise in the Pacific where the people lived in a "state of nature" was by now the talk of Paris. Bougainville had returned to France with a Tahitian named Aotourou, whose innocent charm made him the sensation of the French capital. Part of the philosophy of the Enlightenment was the fascination with the "noble savage," who supposedly lived in the "natural" condition of humanity. In an age of powdered wigs, elaborate fashions, and elegant manners, the myth of "natural" man took on the status of a cult. Before long, Tahiti itself (named New Cythera by Bougainville, after the Greek island where Aphrodite, the goddess of love, rose naked from the sea) became for Europeans an almost mythical place whose inhabitants lived in an Eden of joy and innocence.

Cook had not yet heard of Bougainville's voyage, but he knew that the island would be a source of temptation to his men, who had been cooped up in the small ship for eight months, without female companionship. Wallis had warned that the Tahitians were eager for the strange new things the great ships held—even a common iron nail could bring the favors of a beautiful young woman for a night.

Tahitians' idea of property was radically different from Europeans'; here, a man might claim as his own anything he found. Between the Tahitians' fascination for the hardware of the ship and his own crew's eagerness to take ashore objects to "trade," Cook would have a difficult time keeping the ship's discipline.

No sooner had the *Endeavour* anchored than canoes appeared alongside, loaded with coconuts and other food to trade. Among the first visitors was an elderly man named Owhaa, who had been friendly with the *Dolphin*'s crew and knew many of Cook's officers. Ashore, the men could see islanders waving a friendly welcome.

Cook assembled his men and laid down regulations for the visit. Cook ordered, first, that all were "to cultivate a friendship with the natives and to treat them with all imaginable humanity." Second, no one but those Cook specifically authorized were to trade for food or other ship's provisions. This regulation of trade would keep "prices" from jumping, as the Tahitians discovered that what one man might give a nail or string of beads for, another might be willing to offer an axe or more valuable object. Third, if anyone lost a firearm or work tool or allowed one to be stolen, the value of the lost articles would be deducted from his pay "and he shall receive . . . further punishment." Fourth, similar penalties would be levied on anyone attempting to trade any of the ship's stores. Finally, no iron articles, cloth, "or other useful or necessary articles" were to be traded for anything but provisions.

His precautions were in vain. At a secluded site up the beach, which he named Point Venus, Cook set his men to work building a small fort to protect the men who would have to stay ashore to make the astronomical observations. Leaving armed guards to protect the workmen, Cook and the scientists went inland to explore. After they left an islander grabbed a musket that had been set aside by one of the marine guards at the fort. The other marines opened fire, killing the man who stole the firearm, but another islander picked it up and escaped.

On hearing the shots, Cook returned, and immediately asked Owhaa to gather his people, most of whom had fled. Cook told the remaining islanders that the man had been killed for taking away the musket, and that the English still wished to be friends with the Tahitians.

Parkinson, the artist, was enraged by the killing. He reported in his journal that the English had fired "with the greatest glee imaginable, as if they had been shooting wild ducks. . . . What a pity, that such brutality should be exercised by civilized people upon unarmed ignorant Indians!" He also reported Banks's remark: "If we quarrel with these Indians, we should not agree with angels."

Cook chose to lead his men through example. He asked permission of the islanders before cutting any trees to build the fort. When he heard that one of his men had insulted a native woman, he brought the woman and her husband aboard ship to witness the offender given twelve lashes. The punishment seemed to frighten the woman more than the crew—she tearfully begged for mercy throughout the administration of the lashes to the man.

Cook struggled to make some sense of the islanders' "government." Being English, he tried to interpret the Tahitian political system in the English manner. Among the natives who came aboard ship at his invitation was a man named Tootaha, whom the others paid a good deal of respect. Cook decided this man was the king of the island. (In actual fact, there was no overall chief, but a complicated class system; Tootaha, and the woman named Purea, who had been thought "queen" by the men of the *Dolphin*, were merely members of the highest island class.)

Cook welcomed Tootaha into his cabin, where the "king" was fascinated by the chests and drawers in which Cook stored his belongings. Cook allowed him to open them and examine their contents, and made him a present of a metal adze that he admired.

The fort was completed on the first of May, and Cook ordered it defended with several small cannon and guarded by a garrison of forty-five armed men. "I now thought myself perfectly secure from anything these people could attempt," he wrote, but the very next morning it was found that the astronomical quadrant had been stolen. This was an irreplaceable object, and vitally necessary to the voyage. Banks and Charles Green, the astronomer, began a search and found an islander who told them where it had been taken. Meanwhile, the officers on board the *Endeavour* sighted a canoe carrying Tootaha and took the "king" prisoner.

Cook led a party of armed men to the place where the quadrant had been taken; they recovered it without bloodshed. When Cook returned to the ship, he found Tootaha's people in mourning, for they expected that Cook would execute him. Cook released the "chief," and the thankful Tootaha presented Cook with two hogs.

In the days that followed, the islanders no longer came to trade, and Cook decided to patch things up by bringing gifts to Tootaha's residence. Tootaha, hearing of Cook's intentions, prepared a handsome welcome. Accompanied by Banks and

Solander, Cook was greeted by a huge crowd and the English were invited to remain for a banquet. Part of the entertainment provided was a series of "wrestling matches," as Cook described them, in which the Tahitian men displayed their skills.

Cook's description of the banquet and other island customs showed the keen observation that he would bring to his reports throughout his travels. Much concerned with cleanliness and health, Cook noted that the islanders washed their hands and mouths immediately before and after meals and washed themselves in fresh water three times a day. "The only disagreeable thing about them," he wrote, "is the oil with which they anoint their heads," a coconut oil in which sweet herbs and flowers were mixed.

Cook described the Tahitians as a tall people: "One of the tallest we saw measured six feet three inches and a half." The women wore their hair short, cropped around their ears, while the men "wear it different ways; the better sort let it grow long and sometimes tie it up on the top of their heads or let it hang loose over their shoulders." Both men and women, he noted, plucked out the hair in their armpits "and look upon it as a mark of uncleanliness in us that we do not do the same."

To Cook and his men, one of the most remarkable practices of the Tahitians was the habit of "*tattow* as it is called in their language." Tattooing was then unknown to Europeans, but several of the *Endeavour*'s crew, as well as the artist Parkinson, had themselves tattooed while at Tahiti, perhaps the first sailors to engage in what became a traditional custom of those who work the sea.

Cook and the scientists spent much time ashore; the scientists collected specimens, and Cook began to survey the coast and harbors nearby. On one occasion, Cook and Banks, with one of Tootaha's men as a guide, reached the limits of Tootaha's "territory"; the guide told Cook that the people farther on were at war with Tootaha and would kill them. Cook convinced the guide that English firearms would protect him, and they pushed on. They found the people of the second "kingdom," as Cook called it, to be as friendly as Tootaha's people.

Cook and Banks discovered a number of stone structures, called *maraes*, which were small temples ornamented with carvings and stone totems intended to honor ancestors and gods. *Maraes* marked the burial places of important people. One impressive *marae* was constructed in the shape of a pyramid. Its base was 267 feet by 87 feet, rising in eleven large steps of "coral rock very neatly squared," to a height of 44 feet. On the top stood a wooden carved figure of a bird and near it lay a broken stone figure of a fish. Some large altars near the *marae* were supported by six or eight pillars about 10 feet high. On the altars were the skulls and bones of hogs and dogs and on the beach nearby lay great quantities of human bones.

The discovery of the *maraes* was a significant one. The presence of similar structures throughout the scattered islands of the Pacific would lead Cook to the conclusion that the peoples of these small bits of land in the vast ocean were all descended from one people with a common culture.

The day for the transit of Venus arrived: June 3. Cook stayed with Green and Banks at the main observatory at Point Venus; he sent two other groups to locations nearby to carry out parallel observations, for comparison. It was a brutally hot day, hotter than any so far. Cook recorded a temperature of 119°F.

The purpose of sending Cook's expedition, and others like it, to various points on the globe to make observations of the passage of Venus across the sun was to collate the various observations and through trigonometry to determine the distance from the earth to the sun. To accomplish this, the observations had to be as precise as possible. Unfortunately, the thick atmosphere of Venus made such observations impossible with the degree of precision required. Cook noted the atmosphere "or dusky shade" around the planet when it passed in front of the sun. The haze made the worldwide project a failure.

After the transit, Cook prepared to depart from Tahiti. The men set to work painting and caulking the ship, mending sails, and taking water and wood on board. Yet some aboard had other plans. On June 23, a Portuguese seaman named Manuel Ferrara turned up missing. Cook noted, "I had some reason to think that he was gone with an intent to stay here." The man was soon found, with Tootaha's help; his excuse was that he had been kidnapped.

On July 8, two marines deserted. Cook found that they had taken Tahitian women as wives and had fled into the mountains inland. He seized several "chiefs," including Tootaha, and held them as hostages for the marines' return. On shore, the islanders seized two more of Cook's men in reprisal, but Cook sent a messenger to inform the Tahitians that if any harm came to his men, the chiefs would suffer for it.

All of Cook's men, including the deserters, were returned unharmed, and Cook released the chiefs. The grateful chiefs offered Cook some hogs, but he refused the gift. His anger was reserved for the deserters, and he wrote: "We are likely to leave these people [the Tahitians] in disgust with our behavior towards them, owing wholly to the folly of two of our own people, for it does not appear that the natives had any hand in enticing them away."

Reluctant to leave the islanders with this impression, Cook and Banks went ashore on the thirteenth to make their farewells. The islanders' mood was different from what Cook had expected. They were in tears at the news of the *Endeavour's* imminent departure. Two Tahitians even volunteered to go with the ship as guides: Tupia, a chief and priest, and his servant. Cook knew Tupia was "very intelligent and [knew] more of the geography of the islands situated in these seas, their produce, and the religion, laws, and customs of the inhabitants." Tupia would also prove valuable as an interpreter, and through him Cook and Banks would discover that the languages of many of the peoples of the Pacific were related.

There was no precedent for taking natives on board a ship of the English navy, but Banks offered to be responsible for the expense. Bank's motives were not merely practical—to him Tupia was simply another specimen, not entirely different from the native plants he had collected. Banks wrote in his journal:

> Thank heaven I have a sufficiency [of money] and I do not know why I may not keep him as a curiosity, as well as some of my neighbors do lions and tigers at a larger expense than he will probably ever put me to; the amusement I shall have in his future conversation and the benefit he will be to this ship, as well as what he may be if another should be sent into these seas, will I think fully repay me.

So the *Endeavour* departed with two extra passengers. Cook was proud of the ship's record of health: Two of Banks's servants had died from the cold at Tierra del Fuego, three men had been lost overboard, and the artist Buchan had died of an illness at Tahiti. Not one man had yet died from scurvy, and few even showed symptoms of it.

During the next month, the *Endeavour*, under Tupia's guidance, sailed to several other islands near Tahiti. Cook gave the entire group the name Society Islands, to honor the Royal Society, which had sponsored the voyage. Cook took possession of the islands in the name of the King, but was careful to ascertain the native name of each island whenever possible, and call it by that name on his charts. He prepared the way for other navigators by noting the locations of good harbors, the absence or abundance of fresh water and other supplies, as well as the prevailing winds, currents, and tides.

At last he turned south, carrying out his instructions to search there for the Southern Continent. He searched in vain, as far south as 40°S, finding only a vast and empty sea. The weather grew steadily worse, causing consternation among the less experienced passengers. Parkinson described the situation on September 1:

> We had hard piercing gales and squalls from the west and northwest with violent showers of hail and rain. The sea ran mountain-high, and tossed the ship upon the waves. She rolled so much that we could get no rest, or scarcely lie in bed, and almost every movable on board was thrown down, and rolled about from place to place. In brief, a person who has not been in a storm at sea cannot form an adequate idea of the situation we were in.

The experienced captain had been in many storms and was seldom so florid in description. His entry for the same date reads, "Very strong gales and heavy squalls with rain."

Turning his course to the west, Cook knew he was in the latitude of Tasman's New Zealand, but he did not know the longitude with any certainty. He watched the sea and the air for signs of approaching land. For a time, the only birds in the sky were albatrosses, known for their ability to glide for a thousand or more miles out of sight of land; Banks shot one that measured ten feet eight inches from the tip of one wing to the other. Pieces of floating wood were netted and examined for signs of being new. When Cook noted the color of the sea was paler than usual, he had soundings taken. Heavy swells of water (ocean currents) were carefully noted. Seamen knew that such swells indicated the absence of land in the direction from which they flowed.

Toward the end of September, the men began to sight seaweed and seals. On the twenty-ninth of September, a bird with a short bill, having "the appearance of a land bird," appeared. Finally, on October 7, 1769, at two in the afternoon, a boy on the masthead sighted land. This was the east coast of New Zealand. Cook named the first point of land sighted Young Nick's Head, after Nicholas Young, the twelve-year-old seaman who had made the sighting.

III

THE *ENDEAVOUR* FOUND ANCHORAGE in a bay; on shore there was a small river flowing into the sea. The ship was in need of fresh water, and Banks's eagerness could hardly be restrained, so Cook led a party ashore in two small boats, a pinnace and yawl. The pinnace was left at the mouth of the river while Cook and several others went upstream in the smaller boat. They saw some people on the bank, who fled at their approach. These were Maoris, and Cook knew that four of Tasman's men had died in a Maori attack when the Dutch sailor had visited New Zealand.

Cook's party landed, and he left four men to guard the yawl. The rest accompanied him to a small group of huts. They found there a burned tree stump on which stood a human figurine crudely carved from white pumice stone. It seemed to have a religious significance, and after examination, Cook carefully replaced it with an offering of beads and nails. While examining the huts, Cook's party suddenly heard the sound of shots. They rushed back to the river.

In their absence, four of the Maoris had emerged from the woods. Cook's men guarding the yawl took it downstream toward the pinnace, followed by the Maoris on the bank. The coxswain of the pinnace, seeing what was happening, ordered his men to fire over the heads of the Maoris. This stopped them for a second, but seeing no damage from the noise, one of them prepared to throw his spear at the retreating yawl. The pinnace's men fired two more volleys, killing the man with the spear. The other three Maoris, wrote Cook, "stood motionless for a minute or two, seemingly quite surprised, wondering no doubt what it was that had thus killed their comrade." They dragged his body a little ways off, and then ran.

It was precisely this kind of situation that Cook always tried to avoid. The ship's surgeon examined the man for signs of life. Finding none, the English left nails and beads on the body, and returned to the *Endeavour.*

All through the night, the men of the *Endeavour* could hear shouts and song ashore—whether mourning songs or war chants, the morrow would tell. As the sun rose, Cook again took a party to the river, landing on the bank opposite the huts. The Maoris appeared, and Tupia called out to them in the Tahitian language, saying that they were friends. His speech prompted a kind of war dance, described by Gore:

> About a hundred of the natives, all armed, came down on the opposite side of the river and drew themselves up in lines. Then with a regular jump from left to right and the reverse, they brandished their tongues, and turned up the whites of their eyes, accompanied with a strong, hoarse song, calculated in my opinion to cheer each other and intimidate their enemies.

Before long, however, it was discovered that the Maoris understood some of Tupia's language. He called for them to come across, and finally a man cast off his garment of woven fiber and swam to a rock jutting out of the river. He stood there, gesturing for one of the English to meet him halfway.

Cook immediately gave his musket to one of his men, stripped off his uniform and dove into the water. When he reached the rock, he and the Maori embraced and saluted by touching noses. Cook gave him some trinkets, which the man displayed to his friends. Another of the Maoris swam out to join Cook and his new friend. Cook persuaded the two to swim with him to the shore where the rest of the English waited.

More of the Maoris now began to swim across, though they brought with them the paddle-shaped clubs they called *pattoo-pattoos*. Before long the *Endeavour*'s men were surrounded by Maoris, who picked at their clothes with great curiosity. Though Cook had presents for all, the Maoris seemed not to be fully satisfied and tried to grab the muskets from the marines' hands. Tupia became nervous and told Cook these men "were not our friends."

Finally one of the Maoris tore Green's sword from his belt. Green chased the man to the water's edge, but drew the line at swimming after him. The other Maoris observed the chase with glee, and more people on the opposite shore began to dive into the water. Green drew his pistol and fired it at the thief, apparently killing him. A short battle ensued, during which Cook's men drove off the Maoris by firing at them with "small shot," which could injure but not kill.

A third expedition the following day resulted in more bloodshed. Finally Cook left the bay without getting the fresh water the crew needed. He gave the place the name Poverty Bay, "because it afforded us no one thing we wanted," and reflected on the unhappy encounter in his journal:

I am aware that most humane men who have not expe-rienced things of this nature will censure my conduct in firing upon the people . . . nor do I myself think that the reason . . . will at all justify me. Had I thought that they would have made the least resistance I would not have come near them, but as they did I was not to stand still and suffer either myself or those that were with me to be knocked on the head.

Cook sailed south, facing a coast of sandy beaches, high white cliffs, and inland, high mountains with patches of snow. He had no doubt that this must be the east coast of the land that Tasman had seen in 1642. Tasman had sailed up part of the west coast, but had sailed away without determining whether New Zealand was an island or part of the Southern Continent. Cook's first impulse was to go south to discover the extent of the land, but a few days sailing brought no sight of a suitable landing place. The need for a place where he could replenish his water supply compelled Cook to change course at a point he called Cape Turnagain.

Passing Poverty Bay once again on the journey north, the *Endeavour* soon came to a good anchorage in a bay called Tolaga by the people who lived there. The Maoris of Tolaga Bay were eager to trade for the cloth Cook had obtained from the Tahitians. Cook offered them what he considered better goods, cloth that had been made in England, but the Maoris preferred Tahitian cloth to it. In any case, Cook was delighted to receive in trade wild celery and a plant called scurvy grass. Aboard the *Endeavour*, these were boiled with portable soup and oatmeal. There was no fresh meat available except for a few scraps of dog and rat, both of which were luxury items in the Maoris' diet.

Cook observed the area carefully, recording everything of possible use to later voyagers and colonists. He noted a tree with a deep yellow sap which he thought might be useful for dyes; in fact it was used for that purpose by later generations of

English colonists. His experience as the son of a farm laborer told him that the light and sandy soil inland was suitable for growing root crops. Cook wrote with admiration of the Maoris' "plantations," several acres of ground in which they cultivated sweet potatoes and yams.

Water-casks filled, the *Endeavour* sailed farther north. On October 31, the ship rounded the northeast tip of New Zealand, which Cook dubbed East Cape. Sailing northwest, Cook found harbor in a place he would call Mercury Bay. The transit of Mercury would take place on November 9, and Green wanted to observe it from a base on shore.

While Cook was ashore with Green, Maori canoes approached the ship. The men in them offered to trade a *kakahu*, or woven cloak, for some of the woven cloth aboard. Lieutenant Gore, commanding the ship in Cook's absence, sent the cloth to the natives, but they paddled off quickly without leaving anything in return. Gore fired a musket, killing the man who had taken the cloth. Cook, hearing of the event later, wrote that the punishment was too severe for the crime, "and we had now been long enough acquainted with these people to know how to chastise trifling faults like this without taking away their lives." The fact that even an experienced officer like Gore was willing to fire with little provocation illustrates the kind of policy another sort of commander than Cook might have followed.

Despite Gore's actions, Cook managed to establish good relations with the Maoris at Mercury Bay, and the ship stayed there for another week. Several Maoris accepted Cook's invitation to come on board the *Endeavour*. Among them was a small boy, Te Horeta te Taniwha, who years later told an English visitor his memories of the visit.

Seeing that the English rowed their boats with their backs facing the direction they were going, Te Horeta said, the Maoris decided they were "goblins" with their eyes "at the back of their heads." Te Horeta had a strong memory of Cook, although "His language was [to us] a hissing sound, and the words he spoke were not understood by us in the least." Te Horeta recalled that something in Cook's manner marked him as different:

> There was one supreme man in that ship. We knew that he was the lord of the whole by his perfect, gentlemanly, and noble demeanor. He seldom spoke, but some of the goblins spoke much. But this man did not utter many words: all that he did was to handle our mats and hold our *mere* [spears] and *wahaika* [clubs] and touch the hair of our heads. He was a very good man, and came to us—the children—and patted our cheeks, and gently touched the hair of our heads.

Te Horeta received a nail from Cook as a present.

> I took it into my hand and said *Ka pai* [very good], and he repeated my words, and again patted our heads with his hand and went away. My companions said, "This is the leader of the ship, which is proved by his kindness to us; and also he is so very fond of children. A noble man— a *rangatira*—cannot be lost in a crowd."

The *Endeavour* left Mercury Bay on November 15 and resumed its progress up the coast, stopping frequently, meeting sometimes with friendliness and sometimes with hostility. Where the natives were friendly, Cook could find out the native name for the spot and entered it on his careful chart of the coastline; where they were unfriendly, Cook left without forcing his way ashore; on his chart, these places bear the name of some English place or person.

Cook thought the Maoris "a strong, raw-boned, well-made

active people rather above than under the common size."
Though there seemed to be communication between the
groups living along the coast, they were "too much divided
among themselves to unite in opposing" any British colonists,
although Cook recommended "kind and gentle usage of
them."

With his seaman's eye, Cook admired the canoes and seamanship of the Maoris. They had canoes that could carry sixty
to a hundred people; Cook likened them to New England
whale boats. In fact, whale teeth ornamented the boats, and
some of the islanders' weapons and tools seemed to be made of
whalebone, convincing Cook that the Maoris were capable of
going to sea in these boats and killing the whales that fre-
quented the ocean here.

The arrival of the *Endeavour* commonly brought out from
shore one or more of these large boats, the men inside bran-
dishing their *pattoo-pattoos*, shouting a phrase that Tupia translated as, "Come here, come to shore with us and we will kill you
with our *pattoo-pattoos*." They would leave off their war cry to
accept gifts or engage in trade, and then row off to resume
circling the ship with their war cries and gestures, "in the
doing of which," Cook noted, "they all keep time and motion
together to a surprising degree."

When Cook landed, he found that the Maoris had many
tools for hewing and carving wood. Some of their canoes carried carved figures, most commonly "an oddly designed figure
of a man with as ugly a face as can be conceived, a very large
tongue sticking out of his mouth and large white eyes made of
shells."

The Maoris tilled the soil with wooden spades and planted
and harvested crops. Their most prized tools were axes made
of a green stone, nephrite, which—Cook found later—was
brought from the large southern island. Cook offered "one of

the best axes I had in the ship" for one of these stone axes, but was unable to persuade any Maori to part with one.

The Maoris used musical instruments, described by Cook as trumpets, pipes, and whistles, to accompany their singing and dancing. "Their songs," to Cook, were "harmonious enough but very doleful to a European ear. In most of their dances they appear like madmen, jumping and stamping with their feet, making strange contortions with every part of the body and a hideous noise at the same time."

Cook was not able to find any burial places like those he had seen in Tahiti. He had not yet learned that such places were hidden here, because the Maoris looted the graves of their enemies for bones to make tools and fishhooks. Several times, however, Cook saw people in mourning for loved ones: surviving relatives cut their arms, legs, and chests so deeply that the scars were permanent. Human teeth and fingernails of deceased friends were worn by the living in their honor. In addition to mourning scars, the Maoris also decorated themselves with tattoos, especially in spiral patterns on their faces and buttocks. Older people were virtually covered with scars and tattoos.

Banks, with Tupia's help, was compiling a dictionary listing Tahitian, Maori, and English words side by side. They soon discovered many similarities between the Tahitian and Maori languages.

The farther Cook sailed around the island, the clearer it became that New Zealand was either as large as Britain itself, or the tip of the Southern Continent. In either case, it was a major discovery, and Cook resolved to remain until he had charted the entire coast. It was a task that would keep him there until March 1770.

Early in January 1770, having rounded the northern tip of New Zealand and followed the coastline south, Cook saw a high mountain, which he named Mt. Egmont. He now turned eastward into what he thought was a large bay. In fact, it was the channel that separated the two main islands of New Zealand. Tasman had been here, but had failed to follow the channel through to the opposite side.

Cook found a spacious harbor in the channel, which he named Queen Charlotte's Sound, after the wife of King George III. It was on the north coast of the southern island, and Cook's ships would find it a convenient stopping place many times in the next eight years.

At the harbor, the Maoris greeted the *Endeavour* with a shower of stones hurled from canoes, but Tupia soon convinced them of the English captain's friendly intentions. On the sixteenth, the *Endeavour* was careened, or tipped onto her side, so that the crew could scrape the barnacles off her hull and recaulk the seams between planks that had opened again.

Cook went ashore with a party of men. He wanted to find out if there were any tales of white men having landed here before. He thought this spot was like the place described in Tasman's journal as Murderer's Bay, where several of the Dutchman's crew died in a skirmish with the Maoris.

Rowing toward shore, Cook and his men saw the body of a woman floating in the harbor. On shore, more gruesome sights awaited them. A friendly Maori offered Cook a human armbone "which was quite fresh . . . the flesh had but lately been picked off, which they told us they had eaten." A few days before, the Maoris had captured and eaten the occupants of a passing canoe; the woman in the bay was a passenger who had been overlooked. Nothing so horrified Europeans of Cook's time as the practice of cannibalism, and Cook's disapproval was obvious. The Maoris explained simply that the people in the canoe were strangers. To them, all strangers were enemies.

Cook and his men pretended not to believe the evidence.

Cook told the Maori that the offered armbone was not a human bone, but that of a dog. Cook wrote, "But [the Maori] with great fervency took hold of . . . the flesh of his own arm with his teeth and made a show of eating." Another crewman noted that the Maoris wore the thumbs of their victims in their earlobes as trophies of the hunt. Banks, extending scientific curiosity to a macabre level, purchased the preserved head of a recently killed victim; it still held the hair and skin.

Cook seems to have disregarded the obvious lesson—that, as a stranger, he should be cautious. On January 23, taking along only one other man with a musket, he went inland to climb one of the high hills.

Cook was working on a hunch that the bay he was in led to a channel that divided the north land he had nearly circumnavigated from land to the south. Reaching the top of the hill, he saw the end of the channel to the east: His guess was correct.

On the sixth of February, the repairs to her hull completed, the *Endeavour* set sail again, passing through the channel to the Pacific Ocean on the eastern side of New Zealand on February 8, at a place Cook called Cape Palliser. He turned north and on the following day came once again to the place all recognized as Cape Turnagain. It was proof that they had circled an island.

Cook now turned his course to the south, to find out the extent of the land that lay there. An old man in Queen Charlotte's Sound had told Cook that this too was an island. On the tenth of March, the *Endeavour* reached its southern tip, which Cook named South Cape. By March 26, the ship had circled the southern island and was back in Queen Charlotte's Sound.

The journey around the southern island had been too quick for Banks, who wanted to go ashore frequently to search for specimens. Cook had other purposes. He might have risked a trip ashore if the land had looked suitable for farming or settlement—these concerns always show up in his description of a place. But the southern island was bleak: "No country upon earth," wrote Cook, "can appear with a more rugged and barren aspect than this does from the sea, for as far inland as the eye can reach nothing is to be seen but the summits of these rocky mountains . . . covered in many places with large patches of snow which perhaps have laid there since the creation." Moreover, winter in the Southern Hemisphere was coming on; Cook thought of the safety of his crew and the need for a safe winter harbor.

The dispute between Banks and Cook had reached a flash point on March 14, when Banks demanded that Cook put the ship into the small harbor they were facing on the west coast of the southern island. It was a test as to who was the real commander of the ship, and Cook's will prevailed. From then on, despite his rank, there was no doubt that he was Captain Cook.

Banks was not used to being told no, particularly by the son of a poor farmer, a man who was, by Banks's lights, a nobody. Cook shrugged off the incident, barely mentioning it in his journal, but Banks never forgot it, remembering the day with resentment in a letter as late as 1803.

Safely back in Queen Charlotte's Sound, replenishing his supplies for the trip home, Cook pondered his options. He had looked south of Tahiti for the Southern Continent, and found only islands. Tupia, it was true, had made a chart of other islands, and this would provide a guide for further discoveries. With Tupia's help, Cook and Banks had also found that the languages of the Tahitians and the Maoris were similar; according to Tupia, many other islanders in the Pacific spoke the language. The similarities led Cook to speculate that all the people of the Pacific had a common origin.

Though Cook had settled the question of whether New Zealand was part of the Southern Continent, there was still a vast area of ocean between New Zealand and South America that lay unexplored. The Southern Continent could yet be there. The matter could be cleared up easily, Cook thought, if a ship sailed with the prevailing wind east from New Zealand to Cape Horn. It would not be a difficult journey, by Cook's standards, but not one that he wished to take in a leaky ship with winter coming on.

He therefore decided to sail west. In that direction, Dutch explorers had mapped the west and north coasts of a place they called New Holland, what we know as Australia. Tasman had touched on the southern coast of New Holland at a place he called Van Diemen's Land. (This was the island today called Tasmania.) Cook also knew of Torres's map that showed a strait between New Holland and New Guinea, although that strait was as yet untested by English ships. Even so, if there was no Torres Strait, Cook could sail north of New Guinea to the island of Java, where he could anchor and resupply at the Dutch port of Batavia. From there, he could sail for the Cape of Good Hope and home.

I V

THE JOURNEY ACROSS THE TASMAN SEA was short and uneventful. On the nineteenth of April, Lieutenant Hicks earned a place for his name on Cook's map by being the first to sight the east coast of New Holland. Australia is large enough to be counted as a continent, as Cook's chart would show, but it was not *the* Southern Continent, which was believed to be of much greater extent.

Cook was able to chart the east coast of Australia with great accuracy, thanks to Green's and his own skill with the quadrant and the new lunar tables developed by the British astronomer

Nevil Maskelyne. Sailing north, he recorded every possible aspect of the coast, which was green and woody, with a sparkling white beach of sand. On April 22, people could be seen along the beach. They were of a color so dark that Cook imagined they must be wearing some kind of animal skin. They were aborigines, the native people of Australia, at that time possibly the most primitive people on earth.

On the twenty-ninth, the *Endeavour* sailed into a large harbor, which Cook called Stingray Bay because his men captured several of those large sea animals there. As Cook and his men drew near the beach in a boat, they sighted two men making threatening gestures with their "darts," which were four-pronged sticks tipped with fishbones. Banks cautioned that the darts might be dipped in poison. Cook fired a warning shot; the aborigines replied by flinging stones at the boat. Cook fired a second time, hitting one of the men with small shot; the aborigine picked up a shield and continued to advance.

Finally Cook's boat landed and the aborigines slowly withdrew. The English made their way to a few crude huts, in which they found some small children, to whom Cook gave strings of beads. Three canoes, called by Cook "the worst I think I ever saw" lay on the beach. They were made from a single piece of tree bark, about twelve to fourteen feet long, kept open in the middle by sticks separating the two sides.

The English found fresh water and trees that could make firewood for the ship. In the days that followed, Cook and his men tried to communicate with the shy aborigines. They wore no clothes at all, and were of a dark black color; their only ornamentation was a white pigment with which some of them marked their faces and bodies.

Meanwhile, the scientists were finding a treasure trove of new plants and animals. Separated from other continents for eons, the flora and fauna of Australia had developed their own indigenous forms. Virtually everything that Banks and Solander laid their hands on was unknown to European science. The men of the *Endeavour* were the first Europeans to see a kangaroo. These discoveries caused Cook to rename the place, calling it Botany Bay. Seventeen years later, Britain would begin transporting convicts here, and the city of Sydney was founded just to the north.

Though the natives were primitive, they did not lack for food. The bay abounded with shellfish so numerous that Cook's men scooped armfuls of them out of the water whenever they liked. Cook noticed that the aborigines kept fires in their canoes, apparently for cooking the shellfish.

Banks could have stayed for a much longer time collecting specimens, but Cook wanted to continue his passage north. On May 6, the *Endeavour* left Botany Bay. Before departing, Cook had an inscription cut on one of the trees setting forth the name of his ship and the date. He was laying Britain's claim to a continent.

As the *Endeavour* moved north, Cook began to make what was the longest continuous primary exploration of a coastline ever carried out in a single voyage. Cook sprinkled the map with names of landmarks, bays, capes, inlets, and points. Indeed, he was marking the location and size of the last unexplored inhabitable continent on earth. Some of the names were those of members of the Admiralty: Point Stephens, Cape Hawke, Cape Byron; others were names that described the terrain: Three Brothers, Smoky Cape, Mount Warning (cautioning against the breakers offshore that marked dangerous shoals), Point Danger, Point Lookout, and Bustard Bay, where the *Endeavour* again anchored, on May 23. Cook's stay there was brief, and the natives even shyer than those at Botany Bay. Their crude huts, consisting of little more than bark lean-tos, seemed to be their only possessions. Tupia pronounced them *taata enos,* which Cook translated as "bad or poor people."

Cook sailed on. On the twenty-eighth of May, the *Endeavour* passed a point Cook named Cape Townshend, after another of the Lords of the Admiralty. It was around this point that, unknown to all on board, the *Endeavour* was slipping between the coast of Australia and the Great Barrier Reef, a coral reef that stretches along the coast for about twelve hundred miles.

The Barrier Reef was not visible to Cook, for it is seldom above sea level, but it was a trap for ships caught inside, since its jagged surface can tear through the hull of a ship sailing over it, and breaks in the reef wide enough for a ship to pass through are few and far between. In the south, where Cook reached it, the reef begins more than a hundred miles offshore, but it gradually snakes closer to the coast like the mouth of a funnel, leading a ship toward the place where it must thread a narrow, hazardous path between the coast and the reef. Cook first noticed its presence because of the unusual tides it causes, which caused him to keep men taking soundings throughout each night. A sign of sudden shallows would cause them to shout a warning to the helmsman. Fortunately, the moon was nearly full by this time (the early part of June), and the light helped the *Endeavour*'s helmsman to spot breaking surf that marked the location of the reef.

On the night of the tenth of June, Cook ordered the ship to stand well off the land, where there appeared to be dangerous rocks. Unknowingly, he was steering toward the Barrier Reef. Near nine o'clock that evening, the men taking soundings called out a sudden shift in the bottom: 21 fathoms (120 feet) rapidly gave way to 12, 10, and then 8 fathoms. Cook ordered all hands to their stations, and thought of anchoring for the night, but the water soon deepened again, and "I thought there could be no danger in standing on" (proceeding slowly).

As was his custom, Cook retired to his cabin for the night. The men on watch had been given careful instructions, and the danger seemed over. Cook did not sleep long, for a few minutes before eleven o'clock, the man "in the chains" (taking soundings) called 17 fathoms and "before [he] could heave another cast the ship struck and stuck fast." Banks later recalled feeling two shocks: The ship recoiled off the coral rock, and then pressed forward and struck a second time.

According to Banks, by the time the ship struck the coral the second time, Cook was already on deck in his underclothes, "and he gave his orders with his wonted coolness and precision." A collision of this kind was the worst thing that could happen to the ship, yet Banks was impressed "by the cool and steady conduct of the officers, who, during the whole time, never gave an order which did not show them to be perfectly composed and unmoved by the circumstances, however dreadful they might appear." The crew "worked with surprising cheerfulness and alacrity; no grumbling or growling was to be heard throughout the ship, no, not even an oath."

Cook sized up the situation quickly. The ship was stuck fast on the coral reef. Reports from below indicated that she was not leaking badly. Cook ordered everything aboard that could be spared thrown over the side to lighten the ship to float her free. The immediate danger was of waves and tide carrying the ship farther onto the reef to carve a fatal hole in the hull.

All hands, including the civilians, worked through the night to carry up from the hold the ship's hundreds of casks of fresh water, firewood, iron and stone ballast, stores of food, and even the ship's guns.

Thirteen hours of back-breaking work resulted in the jettisoning of forty to fifty tons of material—to no avail. The tide had gone down, settling the *Endeavour* firmly on the reef. To make matters worse, the ship was now leaking at an alarming rate. There were only four pumps on board, one of which did not work; each had to be hand-operated, and each man, including Cook and Banks, took his turn at operating them.

Half the world away from home, with no way of communicating their plight, every man knew that the loss of the ship meant they would be marooned here forever. By noon of the twelfth of June, Cook had only one hope: At midnight, the tide would be full again and might lift the lightened ship free of the reef.

By nine o'clock that night, the men's hopes rose with the tide, now flooding the reef. The *Endeavour* slowly righted itself.

Now a new and more alarming danger appeared: For the first time, the pumps could not keep up with the leaks in the hull. The water in the hold slowly rose. Worse yet was the possibility that once free of the coral, the ship would take on water even more rapidly. Cook wrote in a rare moment of serious concern: "This was an alarming and, I may say, terrible circumstance and threatened immediate destruction to us as soon as the ship was afloat. However, I resolved to risk all and heave her off."

The ship's boats were sent out carrying five heavy anchors to which strong cables were attached. On board ship, the ends of the cables were wound around the capstan and windlass. When the anchors were set on the bottom, the men strained to turn the capstan and windlass by hand, literally pulling the ship off the reef. It was back-breaking work for a crew that had been working constantly for nearly twenty-four hours, but the effort was successful: at 10:20 the ship floated free.

Cook worked rapidly to plug the leaks so that the ship could search for a harbor. He decided to "fother" the hull. Midshipman Jonathan Monkhouse, who had previous experience in a similar situation, described the task, which Cook assigned him to lead:

> We mix ockham [tar-covered pieces of rope] and wool together . . . and chop it up small and stick it loosely by handfuls all over a [spare] sail and throw over it sheep's

dung or other filth. . . . The sail thus prepared is hauled under the ship's bottom by ropes and if the place of the leak is uncertain it must be hauled from one part of her bottom to another until the place is found where it takes effect; while the sail is under the ship, the ockham, etc. is washed off and part of it carried along with the water into the leak and in part stops up the hole.

The fothering was successful. The leaking soon lessened so that one pump could keep it in check. A general feeling of relief spread through the ship. They had bought time enough to get to an anchorage where the ship could be careened and repaired.

Cook wrote with pride of his crew's response to the danger:

> I must say that no man ever behaved better than they have done on this occasion. . . . Every man seemed to have a just sense of the danger we were in and exerted himself to the very utmost . . . [Monkhouse, in particular, carried out his duties] very much to my satisfaction.

It was the highest praise Cook ever gave.

By July 15, the ship was outside what appeared to be a suitable harbor. The entrance was narrow; guided by two boats, the *Endeavour* tried twice without success to enter. Cook impatiently took his own boat to the harbor entrance and planted buoys marking the channel. On the sixteenth, the ship entered the bay which today bears the name Cook Harbor. It led to an inlet where there was a stream Cook called the Endeavour River.

The ship was hauled up on the beach. Keeping her stern in the water so that she could easily put out to sea again, Cook and his officers waited for low tide so they could inspect the damage to the hull. Several timbers had been sheared through as cleanly as if they had been cut with a saw. Fortunately, a large piece of coral had stuck in the hole, partially plugging it, and the fothering had further closed the opening. The prospects for repair seemed good. The ship's blacksmiths set up a forge ashore and they and the carpenters set to work.

In addition to the work on the hull, new casks would have to be made to replace the ones lost. Provisions were short, and during their stay the men lived mostly on wild yams and sea turtle. Of the yams, Cook wrote, "The tops made good greens and eat exceeding well when boiled, but the roots were so acrid that few besides myself could eat them." Cook's ability to stomach almost any food that came his way became legendary among his crews. Even so, whatever was available was divided equally. Cook remarked, "The meanest person in the ship had an equal share with myself . . . and this method every commander of a ship on such a voyage as this ought ever to observe."

A few curious aborigines made their way from the woods and began to approach the ship. Cook ordered his men to pretend not to notice them until they were close by and then throw presents to them. In this way, he opened an uneasy relationship. Tupia attempted to converse with the aborigines, but their language was unlike any he knew.

After the first contact, the aborigines became more bold. They were fascinated by the turtles that Cook's men brought back from the sea beyond the harbor, and Cook guessed their flimsy vessels would not take them far enough out to catch turtle. Some of the aborigines attempted to carry off a turtle from the ship—not an easy task, since the turtles weighed about 250 pounds—but Cook's men stopped them.

Cook went inland to climb a hill to get a better view of the coast. What he saw "gave me no small uneasiness." As far as he could see were the breakers marking the Barrier Reef; the innermost part was three or four miles away. Clearly, the *Endeavour* could not venture far out to sea, and since the prevailing wind blew from the south, he had no alternative but to sail north and attempt to find a passage through the reef farther up.

Six weeks went by, and the *Endeavour* was judged seaworthy again. Molyneux, the master, had traveled up the coast in a boat and reported that there was no safe passage there, even along the coast. Nevertheless, it was the only direction Cook could sail, and he was impatient. He wrote, "Laying in port spends time to no purpose, consumes our provisions of which we are very short in many articles, and we have yet a long passage to make to the East Indies through an unknown and perhaps dangerous sea."

Again Cook personally laid the buoys that marked the channel out of the bay. On August 4, the *Endeavour* set out, "warping" her way—the boats laying anchors ahead of the ship and the muscle power of men at the capstan literally pulling it forward. This was the most arduous work—it often took three hours just to raise the anchor with its 150-fathom cable from the bottom. Yet the wind blew so strongly that if the sails were raised, the ship would move too swiftly for the helmsman to keep it from blowing onto the shoals.

On the eleventh of August, the petty officer at the masthead called down a warning: The land ahead extended across their path, meeting the islands and reef to the east. The ship, seemingly, had reached a dead end. Cook climbed to the masthead for a look. In his judgment, what the officer had seen as mainland to the north was a chain of islands.

Practically everyone disagreed, including Molyneux, who made his own observations from the masthead. Cook went ashore in a boat to see better, and saw what he felt was a passage through the islands and past the reef to open sea. On the fourteenth, following his own judgment, Cook was proved right and the *Endeavour* sailed with surprising ease through the reef.

Unfortunately, the seas beyond the reef beat against the ship with greater force, and the leaks began again. At least one pump had to be kept going continually. Furthermore the wind, blowing west, kept forcing the *Endeavour* back toward the jagged coral. At daybreak on the sixteenth, the breakers marking the reef could be seen less than a mile away.

In desperation, Cook sent the yawl and longboat into the water (the pinnace was under repair) to tow the ship. The ship's "sweeps" (large oars used at the stern in emergencies) were also brought into play, but by 6:00 A.M. the ship was only eighty to a hundred yards from the breakers.

On the sea side, the coral reef sank at an almost perpendicular angle into the ocean, so there was no bottom reachable by the anchor's cable to hold the ship. This was the most dangerous moment since the night and day the *Endeavour* had spent with a smashed bottom on the reef two months earlier. This time, the nearest land was ten leagues off and the boats would not carry all the ship's crew and passengers. "Yet in this truly terrible situation," Cook wrote, "not one man ceased to do his utmost and that with as much calmness as if no danger had been near." The waves breaking on the reef were "mountains high" and the ship would certainly be broken to pieces there, only "a dismal valley, the breadth of one wave" away.

In this extremity, Cook's luck brought a small air of wind, but it was enough to fill the sails and cause the ship to move slowly away from the reef. It was a brief respite, for after ten minutes the breeze died and the ship began to drift toward the reef again. Now, however, an opening in the reef was sighted, only as wide as the length of the ship. It was a small chance, but their only one, and the boats strained to pull the *Endeavour* through the opening.

Just as the ship reached the reef, the ebb tide began with unusual force, gushing out through the opening in the reef, and sweeping the ship out to sea. By noon the *Endeavour* was nearly two miles away from the reef, yet still within the grip of its tide. But the flow of the tide now changed, and began to pull the *Endeavour* once more toward the coral.

This time, a larger opening in the reef was sighted, and the helmsman guided the ship toward it. The full force of the flood tide swept the *Endeavour* through the opening like a twig in a fast-flowing river.

Ironically the crew of the *Endeavour* now found themselves safe within the reef "which but two days ago our utmost wishes were crowned by getting clear of."

As Cook decided what course to follow next, his journal entry gives a rare indication of his thought processes. He mused about the "vicissitudes attending this kind of . . . unknown navigation. . . . Were it not for the pleasure which naturally results to a man from being the first discoverer . . . this service would be insupportable." Cook, in a dangerous situation far from help, showed his awareness of the thin line between success and failure. If a man failed to explore an unknown coast because of danger, "he is then charged with timorousness and want of perseverance, and at once pronounced the unfittest man in the world to be employed as a discoverer." On the other hand, if "he boldly encounters all the dangers and obstacles he meets and is unfortunate enough not to succeed," he would then be called reckless and unfit for the trust of command.

Cook knew that no one could justly call him timid, and he would not be thought too bold, "if I am fortunate enough to surmount all the dangers we may meet." He admits to having taken more risks than he should have, "but if I had not we should not have been able" to chart the coastline.

These thoughts seemed to clear Cook's mind of doubt: His justification would lie in completing the charting of the coast, and in finding the rumored passage between New Guinea and New Holland (Australia), if it existed. The only way to accomplish this task was to stay within the reef, and let danger be hanged. He set sail for the north, sending the boats far ahead of the ship to take soundings, and assigning "a good lookout" to the masthead.

The soundings were very irregular, but in three days the *Endeavour* reached a point that Cook judged to be the northern tip of New Holland. He landed there, naming the spot York Cape, and with Banks and Solander climbed the highest hill he could find. In the waters to the northwest, he saw what he judged to be a string of islands. There must be a passage through them to the west that would enable the *Endeavour* to sail between Australia and New Guinea. He formally took possession of the east coast of New Holland in the name of the King of England, George III, and hoisted the British flag. The men with him fired a volley of three shots, which were answered by the men on the *Endeavour* in the harbor far below. His actions would result in England's acquisition of a continent.

Cook's eye was sure; he navigated the tricky tides that for centuries had baffled voyagers coming from the opposite direction, and by late afternoon of August 23, the *Endeavour* cleared the waters that were known as Torres Strait. The way was clear to the Dutch port on Java.

The captain had only two regrets: that he had sailed for a few days beyond the reef, leaving a gap on his chart of the Australian coastline, and that he had not found the northern limit of the Barrier Reef, which extends north of Torres Strait. But even Cook had his limits: "This was a thing I had neither time nor inclination to go about, having been already sufficiently harassed with dangers without going to look for more."

Dampier had described the west coast of New Holland as barren and miserable. On the east coast, Cook found "all such things as nature has bestowed upon it in a flourishing state." He believed that grain, fruit, roots, and agricultural products of all kinds could be planted and grown there.

As he sailed toward Batavia, toward what he regarded as a safe harbor, Cook mused in his journal about the people of the coast he had just mapped. His final word on the Australian aborigines marks another kind of breaking point. Cook's intellectual progress had carried him almost as far as the journey from the farm where he was born to the wider world of London and finally to unexplored coasts. With little formal education, he had absorbed the intellectual achievements of Enlightenment Europe. Now he was attempting to comprehend the ways of a people who were completely outside the European experience:

They may appear to some to be the most wretched people on earth, but in reality they are far more happier than we Europeans; being wholly unacquainted not only with the superfluous but the necessary conveniences so much sought after in Europe, they are happy in not knowing the use of them. They live in a tranquility which is not disturbed by the inequality of condition. The earth and sea of their own accord furnishes them with all things necessary for life. They covet not magnificent houses, household-stuff, etc. They live in a warm and fine climate and enjoy a very wholesome air, so that they have very little need of clothing. . . . In short they seemed to set no value upon anything we gave them, nor would they ever part with anything of their own for any one article we could offer them. This in my opinion argues that they think themselves provided with all the necessarys of life.

Cook's opinion was not the same as the Enlightenment view of the "natural savage," for he did not attribute to the aborigines virtues and values that they didn't have. He was trying to see them by their own terms, and not by European standards.

The trip to Batavia was uneventful. Cook acknowledged that everyone but he, Banks, and Solander was "now pretty far gone with the longing for home." His greatest satisfaction was that the ship was free from disease—proving the effectiveness of Cook's attempts to promote proper diet and clean conditions aboard.

But Batavia proved to be an unhealthy place. Cook reached there on October 11, only to face administrative difficulties over the repairing and reprovisioning of his ship. When the *Endeavour* was overturned, the damage done on the reef was found to be far worse than anyone thought. It would require a long stay for repairs. Only two weeks after their arrival, however, the men began falling sick. Cook sent them ashore for proper care, but the disease, which was malaria, had its origins ashore.

The sick list grew. Cook himself fell victim to the malaria and dysentery that infected the port. He recovered, but many did not. Among the dead were Tupia and his servant; Cook blamed himself for taking the innocent islanders on the ship.

Taking additional crew to man the ship, Cook left Batavia on December 26. But the *Endeavour* carried the diseases with her. Cook's journal from Batavia to the Cape of Good Hope, which the *Endeavour* reached on the fifteenth of March, reads like a long obituary.

Among the dead were Solander's assistant, Spöring; Parkinson; the astronomer Green; the surgeon William Monkhouse and his brother, Midshipman Jonathan Monkhouse, one of Cook's most trusted men. Back in England Cook would have the sad task of writing to their aged father.

Fear gripped the ship. Cook mentions a crew member who had

long tended upon the sick and enjoyed a tolerable degree of health. One morning coming upon deck he found himself a little griped [the first stage of dysentery] and immediately began to stamp with his feet and exclaim "I have got the gripes, I have got the gripes, I shall die, I shall die." In this manner he continued until he threw himself into a fit and was carried off the deck in a manner dead. However he soon recovered and did very well.

Cook reached the Cape of Good Hope, took on more men there, and set out on the last leg of the journey, up the coast of Africa toward home. He encountered a ship that had recently left England, and learned from the captain that the long absence of the *Endeavour* had given rise to newspaper stories speculating on her fate. The betting was heavy that she had sunk to the bottom with all hands.

Cook overcame the odds, and on July 13, 1771, the *Endeavour* reached the mouth of the Thames. Cook left her there in charge of a river pilot and traveled overland to London. He was to meet the King.

CHAPTER THREE

Resolution AND Adventure, 1772-1775

I

FOLLOWING ORDERS from the Admiralty to keep the voyage secret, Cook confiscated the journals of his officers and men shortly before their arrival in England. However, the ebullient Banks soon made public the *Endeavour*'s spectacular scientific and geographical discoveries. The newspapers were full of stories about the voyage, and Banks and Solander became celebrities. Cook's contribution was noted but not so celebrated; he had navigated the ship, but the scientific discoveries, according to the newspapers, were the work of Banks and Solander.

Cook never sought celebrity. He reported to the Admiralty and turned over his log and those of his men. The Lords of the Admiralty were fully aware of Cook's contribution, and indicated their approval by arranging his introduction to the King. But the Admiralty was wary of revealing too much about Cook's real achievement—the charts he had made. They might give too much information to the French, and it was known that Bougainville was planning a second expedition, to establish a French settlement at Tahiti and continue the search for the Southern Continent.

Cook laid before the Admiralty his own plan for a second voyage, entering the Pacific from the west and sailing in a high latitude toward South America in search of the Southern Continent. If there was none to be found, the voyage could turn toward discovering the islands on Tupia's map. By the end of September 1771, the Earl of Sandwich, now First Lord of the Admiralty, had given instructions for the purchase of two more ships for a second voyage.

Meanwhile Cook had returned to his family in Mile End, finding that a third son had been born, and had died, in his absence, and that his four-year-old daughter had also died. We shall never know what these sorrows meant to Cook, for his sea journals never mention his family. We know only that he spent as much time ashore with them as he could, and that he had the normal ambition for his children—he placed the names of his first two sons on his muster books for the later voyages, so that they could "earn" seniority in sea time in the navy—a common practice of the time.

Cook and his wife went up to Ayton to help his seventy-seven-year-old father move to the home of one of Cook's sisters. He also visited his old master, John Walker, whose family gave him a reception befitting one of their own who had returned home after great exploits. Cook's letters to the Walkers are warmer than his journals and show a justifiable pride in what he had accomplished. The private acclaim of these few friends and family were sufficient for Cook.

There was work for Cook to do. The Admiralty had no doubt as to who should command the second voyage, and Cook had charge of procuring and refitting the ships. Like the *Endeavour*, they had been built for the coal trade. They were

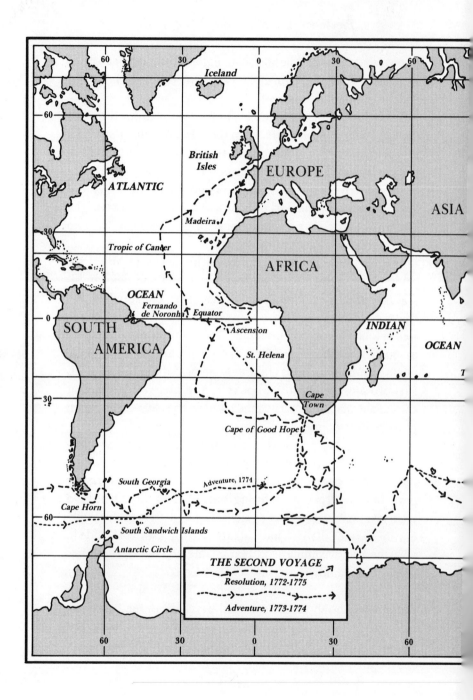

THE SECOND VOYAGE
Resolution, 1772-1775
Adventure, 1773-1774

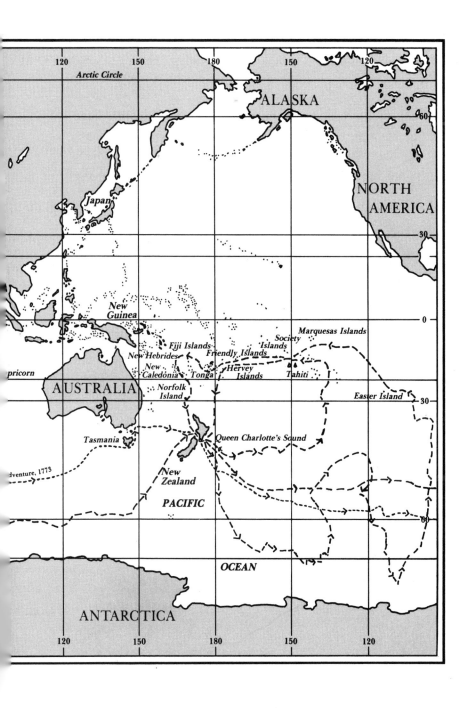

given the names *Drake* and *Raleigh*; then, after consideration that these famous English names might be offensive to the Spanish, they were renamed the *Resolution* and the *Adventure*.

The scientific successes of the *Endeavour* produced many new suggestions for the second voyage. In navigation Cook had shown that the use of a quadrant with Maskelyne's lunar tables could determine longitude with great accuracy. But the lunar tables were cumbersome and time-consuming; though Cook had taught his junior officers to use them, a far simpler method of determining longitude would result if a timepiece could be developed to keep time accurately at sea. The timepiece would be set for the time in England (later standardized as the exact time at Greenwich, England), and a simple comparison with the time at sea (obtained by calculating the angle of the sun in the sky) would give the longitude of the ship.

But it had so far proved impossible to make a timepiece that would remain accurate under varying conditions of humidity and temperature, plus the rolling of the ship. As long ago as 1714 the British Board of Longitude had offered a large cash prize for the invention of such a timepiece. In 1764, a time-piece made by an English watchmaker, John Harrison, had been tested on two voyages to the Americas. Harrison claimed the prize, but had been awarded only half of it because the Admiralty felt that the "watch" (it was actually a large chronometer that could be mounted on deck) had not been fully tested. The voyage Cook proposed would be a harsh test of a copy of Harrison's chronometer, as well as three other chronometers devised by John Arnold.

The ships would carry other experimental inventions. Cook requested "warping machines," which were designed to relieve the crew of the kind of back-breaking labor the men of the *Endeavour* had gone through to pull the ship off the Great Barrier Reef. In addition there were several devices intended to distill fresh water from sea water. Many additional antiscorbutics were also proposed, and among those Cook stored aboard were "inspissated," or condensed, beer, marmalade of carrots, "rob" of oranges and lemons, and salted cabbage, as well as Cook's standard, sauerkraut.

After it became known that he was to command the second voyage, Cook received invitations to the gatherings of London intellectual society. Among those who welcomed Cook was Dr. Charles Burney, a musician who had a bright and lively circle of friends. His brilliant daughter Fanny thought Cook was rather aloof from the company. As she remembered:

> This truly great man appeared to be full of sense and thought; well-mannered, and perfectly unpretending; but studiously wrapped up in his own purposes and pursuits; and apparently under a pressure of mental fatigue when called on to speak, or stimulated to deliberate, upon any other.

Dr. Burney did, however, succeed in his suggestion that his twenty-one-year-old son James should accompany Cook on the next voyage.

Cook's lack of interest in the intellectual society of London, and his inexperience, led him to agree to another proposal that came from Lord Sandwich. The writer Dr. John Hawkesworth was to be given the task of assembling the journals of Byron, Wallis, Carteret, Banks, and Cook into a long work known as Hawkesworth's *Voyages.* The sale of the book would bring Hawkesworth almost as much as the salaries of the four captains whose work he used. But Cook, for one, was highly embarrassed when he saw the book (after his second voyage), which was full of inaccuracies and absurdities credited to Cook's hand.

The worst difficulties Cook faced before the second voyage began were those presented by Banks. Banks, only twenty-eight, had experienced sudden fame that brought him acclaim throughout Europe. Many eminent scientists wrote to ask his advice, make suggestions for new discoveries, and even to request that he allow them to go along on the new voyage—as if the decision were Banks's to make.

Banks had grandiose plans. He thought it might be possible for the ship to reach the South Pole itself, and speculated in a letter, "O how glorious would it be to set my heel upon the Pole! and turn myself round 360 degrees in a second." Banks planned to travel in style, and recruited a whole company of scientists, artists, servants, and even entertainers to go on the voyage.

Cook generously agreed to give up the captain's cabin completely for Banks's personal use; other quarters, less convenient, were constructed for Cook on the *Resolution*. Then at last another whole deck was added to the ship to accommodate Banks's retinue. Banks ordered and paid for tons of scientific equipment. Room for all this had to be found; more stowage space was added to the *Resolution*.

All these preparations delayed the start of the voyage, but when the refitted and rebuilt *Resolution* began its preliminary trip down the Thames, the pilot reported it was so top-heavy that it was in danger of capsizing in the comparatively calm river. Clerke, who was to go as second lieutenant, wrote Banks: "By god, I'll go to sea in a grog tub, if required, or in the *Resolution* as soon as you please; but must say I think her by far the most unsafe ship I ever saw or heard of."

Cook had to remain more discreet, since Banks was a personal friend of Lord Sandwich. Cook let the matter be known to his old ally, Palliser, who was by now the Comptroller of the Navy. After Palliser inspected the ship, he ordered it put back in dry dock for adjustments. The extra captain's quarters and deck were removed. Banks would have to make his expedition fit the ship, not the other way around.

John Elliott, a fourteen-year-old midshipman aboard the *Resolution*, described in his journal the scene when Banks arrived to see the restoration taking place. Banks, he wrote, "swore and stamped upon the wharf like a madman, and instantly ordered his servants and all his things out of the ship." Banks went so far as to appeal to the Admiralty for new ships, but Cook had already written of the *Resolution*, "She was the ship of my choice and . . . I thought the fittest for the service she was going upon of any I had ever seen."

Banks went a step further and suggested there were other commanders who could do a better job than Cook. At this, even Sandwich turned his back on Banks. Finally Banks went his own way, outfitting an expedition to Iceland, and passes from the story of Cook.

There was still a need for scientists aboard, and the man selected to head the group was a Prussian named John Reinhold Forster. He was well educated, but his quarrelsome habits had lost him a succession of teaching posts. The bad-tempered Forster would prove a trial to Cook during the voyage. Forster's brilliant son George also accompanied the voyage, and one of his main tasks seems to have been to mediate an uneasy peace between his father and the rest of the ship's company.

The commander of the *Adventure* was Captain Tobias Furneaux, who had gone around the world with Wallis on the *Dolphin*. He had effectively commanded the ship when his superiors were ill, and came with the highest recommendation.

On Cook's ship, the *Resolution*, were several officers who possessed Cook's spark, and would themselves become famous. Cook had been promoted to full captain, and his first lieutenant was Robert Palliser Cooper, a relative of Cook's patron, Navy Comptroller Hugh Palliser. He was eventually to become a rear admiral. Charles Clerke, who refused Banks's offer to go on the expedition to Iceland, would later command his own ship on Cook's third voyage. The third lieutenant, Richard

Pickersgill, was frequently trusted by Cook to be the first to encounter new islanders. Young Elliott, in his frank way, described Pickersgill as "a good officer . . . but liking ye grog."

Preparations complete at last, the two ships proceeded to Plymouth harbor, their departure point. Cook discovered he had five men sick. Discharging them, he asked the commander of the port for one volunteer from each of the five other ships then in the port. Whether they were truly volunteers or not, the five extra men soon scrambled over the side of the *Resolution*, little knowing that a three-year voyage around the world awaited. Their names were duly entered in Cook's muster book, earning them a place in the history of the sea. Such was the uncertain life of British seamen in the eighteenth century.

Finally, with 112 officers and men and 6 civilians aboard the *Resolution*, and 83 aboard the *Adventure*, the vessels departed from England on the thirteenth of July, 1772. Cook's chief instruction was to clear up once and for all the theory of the Southern Continent. To accomplish the task, he was equipped with imperfectly mapped descriptions of previous discoveries that purported to be part of the continent. Among these was the Cape Circumcision that French sailor Jean-Baptiste Bouvet had found in the far South Atlantic in 1739. Bouvet was enthusiastic in describing the place as part of the Southern Continent, but his charting of it was wildly off, and no one had found it since.

There was no possibility of circling the globe in a high latitude in a single season. The weather there would be bad enough in midsummer, and Cook would have to find his way north to a milder climate during the Southern Hemisphere's winters. After putting in at the Cape of Good Hope, he would spend the early part of 1773 probing the Antarctic. Then he would resupply in New Zealand and spend the middle part of the year in the South Pacific. The second polar cruise would come in late 1773 and early 1774. Following this, there would be another series of discoveries in the South Pacific. Finally, Cook was to complete his survey of the far southern parts of the globe in early 1775.

II

THE VOYAGE FROM PLYMOUTH to Cape Town took three months. For some, such as young Elliott, it was a training cruise. Elliott wrote:

> In the early part of the voyage, Capt. Cook made all us young gentlemen do the duty aloft the same as the sailors, learning to hand and reef the sails, and steer the ship, exercise small arms, etc., thereby making us good sailors as well as good officers.

"Young gentlemen" such as Elliott were following in the tradition of upper-class English families whose younger sons found careers at sea. They were sent at an early age because it was believed they would thus become accustomed to the hardships of life on ship more easily. Though they had sailor's rank, these young gentlemen were destined for eventual promotion to officers. Those who learned their seamanship under Cook acquired a reputation for being exceptional sailors and officers. When one such young gentleman came for his oral examination, the committee of older officers noted that he had served with Cook; the older men then merely engaged him in conversation for a while and passed him without further ado.

Some of the experimental foods and equipment soon proved of little value. The machines intended to turn salt water into fresh did not work well. This was a particularly unpleasant surprise, because Cook had brought a fair number of hogs, goats, fowl, and cattle on board to distribute among the South Sea Islanders, and the livestock had increased the ship's need for water. After the usual stop at Madeira, Cook was compelled to put in at the Cape Verde Islands to replenish the ship's water supplies.

At Cape Town, which the ships reached on October 30, there was an opportunity to take the chronometers ashore to test their reliability. The copy of Harrison's was keeping accurate time, while Arnold's "watch" on the *Resolution* was more than an hour and a half off. One of Arnold's other two models on the *Adventure* was doing somewhat better, but the other stopped and could not be restarted.

At Cape Town, Forster met a young man from Sweden, Anders Sparrman. Sparrman had been a pupil of Linnaeus, and Forster highly recommended the young man to Cook. He was added to the *Resolution*'s company.

Cook heard news of two French explorers while he was at the Cape. The French were quickly seeking to follow up on Bougainville's discoveries, and evidently were ahead of Cook. The first captain, Marion du Fresne, had been assigned to return the Tahitian whom Bougainville had brought to France, but the islander had died before the ship reached the Cape in December, 1771. Cook, remembering Tupia and his servant, was saddened. "Had any one of these three persons lived to return," Cook wrote, "they must have prepossessed the islanders . . . very much in favor of Europeans." Now, returning without their "passengers," the Europeans might be thought of as kidnappers or slavers.

The other French voyage was commanded by Yves-Joseph

de Kerguelen, who had already returned to the Cape with the news of land in the Indian Ocean, far to the southeast of the Cape of Good Hope. Like Cape Circumcision, Kerguelen's Land eventually proved to be an isolated speck of land, but Kerguelen described it as the gateway to "a fifth part of the world." He sketched out the glorious possibility of France's colonization and exploitation of this land. Unfortunately, his chart showed the position of the island nearly five degrees west of its true location—such was the state of navigation in most of Europe at the time Cook was making his remarkably accurate charts.

By the time Cook heard of his voyage, du Fresne already lay dead, a victim of a Maori attack in New Zealand. Not knowing this, Cook felt there was need for haste. He left Cape Town on November 22, sailing almost due south. The men put on their fearnought trousers and jackets, and soon the cold weather was upon them, accompanied by gale winds and storms.

On December 9, penguins made their appearance; the following day, there was frost on the sails and decks and snow and sleet in the early morning. Some of the livestock had already died from the cold, giving the crew a feast of hogs, sheep, and poultry that had been intended for the South Sea Islanders.

At latitude 50°40′S, the ships sighted an "island of ice"—an iceberg. William Wales, astronomer on the *Resolution*, had seen similar ice islands in Hudson Bay, but he thought these in the south were different in that the tops and sides were smooth and straight. They were twice as high as the highest mast on the *Resolution*. Burney described them: "When the sun shines and the sky is clear they are of a fine light blue and transparent; in bad, dirty weather they resemble land covered with snow, the lower part appearing black." In fact, the ships' lookouts frequently mistook them for land.

The number of ice islands increased, and the ships sailed an uneasy course among them. An unfavorable wind might at any time smash a ship to splinters against an ice island, and the cold weather coated the ropes with ice, made the sails brittle, and numbed the men's hands. Orders to shift sail to avoid danger could not be carried out quickly. Even Cook wrote, "when one reflects on the dangers . . . the mind is filled with horror."

On December 14, the ships encountered a solid field of ice that blocked their way to the south. The crew discovered that ice chipped from the pack could be melted into fresh water. To Cook it was a welcome source of water, but it also indicated to him that the ice had been formed on land, rather than from sea water.

The ships edged their way along the ice pack to the south and east. On the morning of December 15, Cook reported four inches of snow on the deck, the temperature around 27°F, and the "rigging and sails all decorated with icicles."

On December 21, there was a break in the ice, and Cook set a southerly course again, "the course I now intend to steer till I meet with interruption," he wrote with some determination.

Christmas arrived. The crew had been saving their grog for days in anticipation, and Cook allotted them an extra ration to aid the celebration. Opinions differed on the men's conduct. Cook: "Mirth and good humor reigned throughout the ship." Forster: "Savage noise and drunkenness."

On New Year's Day, 1773, the ships sailed across the 60th parallel south. They were far off any reliable maps, with the ships in continual danger from collision with the ever-present icebergs. At about noon on January 17, the *Resolution* and *Adventure* crossed the Antarctic Circle. They were, Cook noted, "undoubtedly the first and only ships that ever crossed that line."

The next day, thirty-eight ice islands were counted within sight of the ships, and soon afterward another vast field of pack ice was sighted. Cook himself climbed the masthead to observe:

> I could see nothing to the southward but ice, in the whole extent from east to WSW . . . of such extent that I could see no end to it. . . . I did not think it was consistent with the safety of the sloops or any ways prudent of me to persevere in going farther to the south as the summer was already half spent and it would have taken up some time to have got round this ice.

The ships turned north, but on the eighth of February, a thick fog descended. The ships became separated. Cook began firing one of the *Resolution*'s guns at regular intervals, but the ice islands were breaking up all around, making loud cracking noises that were similar to those of the guns. After two days' search, Cook decided that he would count on meeting Furneaux at the prearranged rendezvous in Queen Charlotte's Sound. He made for New Zealand, keeping far south as long as possible, but encountered no land.

On March 25, the *Resolution* sighted New Zealand. Cook anchored off the southwest coast to give his crew some rest and possibly fresh fruit and vegetables. It had been 117 days since the men of the *Resolution* had seen land.

It was a good choice for a stopping place. Dusky Bay, as Cook called it, abounded in food, water, and wood. Unarmed, Cook approached three islanders—a man armed with a staff and two women who held spears "not less than 18 feet in length,"—and persuaded them to put aside their weapons. The people presented Cook with some cloth and a green stone *pattoo-pattoo*, a generous gift as the captain well knew, since he had not been able to persuade any Maoris to part with one on his earlier voyage.

Cook's confidence in dealing with strange peoples often appears more than a little reckless. While exploring a river that flowed into the bay, he encountered another group of people carrying spears. Cook waded ashore to greet them, waving his men back into the boat. He described his reception:

> at length one of them laid down his spear, pulled up a grass plant and came to me with it in his hand, giving me hold of one end while he held the other; standing in this manner he made a speech not one word of which I understood. In it were some long pauses, waiting, as I thought, for me to make answer, for when I spoke he proceeded. As soon as this ceremony was over . . . we saluted each other. He then took his *hahou*, or coat, from off his back and put it upon mine, after which peace seemed firmly established. More of our people joining us did not in the least alarm them.

The *Resolution*, now shipshape and with a rested crew, left Dusky Bay on the eleventh of May and made its way up the coast to Queen Charlotte's Sound. On the morning of the nineteenth, the welcome sight of the *Adventure* greeted Cook, and Furneaux came aboard to deliver the log of his journey.

After losing sight of the *Resolution*, Furneaux had quickly drawn away from the ice. On the way to New Zealand he had passed by the land that Tasman called Van Diemen's Land. Furneaux had moored offshore to chart the part of the coastline he could see, but he failed to discover it was in fact a large island—today called Tasmania.

William Bayly, astronomer aboard the *Adventure*, confided to his own journal his doubts about Furneaux's ability as a commander. Bayly had wanted to take a boat ashore at Van Diemen's Land, but received "evasive refusals" from Furneaux, who was reluctant to take chances with the natives ashore. Even at Queen Charlotte's Sound, where Cook had earlier established good relations with the Maoris, Furneaux avoided close contact with them. Furthermore, he had not enforced Cook's rule that the men be provided with meals of scurvy grass, celery, and other fresh vegetables found there. Furneaux confined his activity to planting an English vegetable garden ashore. Cook lost no time in seeing to it that the crew of the *Adventure* began eating the foods Cook knew would keep them free from scurvy.

The Maoris, recognizing Cook, now gave him a warm welcome. They asked after their friend Tupia, the Tahitian who had been with Cook earlier, and mourned at the news that he had died. Cook led the Maoris to the gardens Furneaux had planted, and explained how they were to be tended and harvested. One man "was so pleased with them that he immediately began to hoe the earth about the plants."

In similar circumstances, other Maoris had killed Tasman and du Fresne, and later at this same spot would massacre some of Furneaux's crew, when he reappeared without Cook. Cook's success with native peoples was due in part to his perceptiveness at understanding their customs. The men of the *Adventure* reported that the Maoris were willing to sell their own children for trinkets, but soon Cook found out the truth of the matter:

. . . the report took rise [because the *Adventure*'s crew] were utter strangers to their language and customs. It was not uncommon for [the Maoris] to bring their children with them aboard and present them to us in expectation of our making them presents. This story, though extremely trifling in itself, will show how liable we are to mistake these people's meaning and to ascribe to them customs they never knew even in thought.

Cook was already noting the changes that contact with Europeans brought to native cultures. Known today to cultural anthropologists as "diffusion," this phenomenon makes the keen observations of Cook—who was often the first or nearly the first European to observe the Pacific peoples—particularly important in ascertaining the original cultures.

Cook noticed that on his earlier visit, the Maori women would occasionally sleep with the men of the *Endeavour*, but generally "in a private manner and without the [Maori] men seeming to interest themselves in it." On this trip, the attitude of the Maoris had changed: Now the Maori men were the "chief promoters of this vice and for a spike nail . . . will oblige their wives and daughters to prostitute themselves whether they will or no and that not with the privacy decency seems to require."

Cook vigorously condemned his own crew for their part in promoting this change. His reflections are hardly those of a happy conquerer, who presumes himself superior:

> Such are the consequences of a commerce with Europeans and what is still more to our shame, civilized Christians. We debauch their morals . . . and we introduce among them wants and perhaps diseases which they never before knew and which serves only to disturb that happy tranquility they and their forefathers had enjoyed. If anyone denies the truth of this assertion, let him tell me what the natives on the whole extent of America have gained by the commerce they have had with Europeans.

III

FURNEAUX NOW RECEIVED a rude shock: He expected that Cook would spend the winter here in rest before returning to the Antarctic the following year. In fact, Cook did not intend to "idle away the whole winter in port. . . . I proposed to Captain Furneaux to spend that time in exploring the unknown parts of the sea to the east and north." Cook wanted to use Tupia's map, which showed many islands as yet unvisited by Europeans. He was far too restless and eager for discovery to remain idle.

By June 8, the ships were out of the strait and at sea again, bound for Tahiti. Cook's plan was to use the island as a base where he could obtain supplies.

On August 15, the ships sighted Tahiti. Cook gave instructions to his officer of the deck to sail for an anchorage on the southeast side of the island. But when the captain arose on the morning of the sixteenth, he discovered that the course had not been properly followed and that the *Resolution*, with the *Adventure* following, was now in danger of being blown onto a rocky shore. The crews of both ships spent a frantic day using small boats to pull the ships clear.

Sparrman, though showing his prudish nature, gives an interesting portrayal of Captain Cook under pressure:

I drew no small satisfaction from . . . the celerity and the lack of confusion with which each command was executed to save the ship. . . . I should have preferred, however, to hear fewer "goddamns" from the officers and particularly the captain, who, while the danger lasted, stamped about the deck and grew hoarse with shouting. I have sailed with captains capable of imposing the most perfect obedience and the most delicate maneuvers without swearing.

But another, seldom seen, side of Cook appears in Sparrman's account:

> As soon as the ship was once more afloat, I went down to the ward room with Captain Cook who, although he had from beginning to end of the incident appeared perfectly alert and able, was suffering so greatly from his stomach that he was in a great sweat and could hardly stand.

Cook planned to stay at Tahiti only long enough to obtain fresh food and water. He discovered that Tootaha, the "king" of the island, had died in a battle. There were several who now claimed his place. One was Otoo, an imposing man of about thirty years of age, six feet three inches in height. Otoo seemed very afraid of the ship's guns, and refused Cook's invitation to come on board. Cook thought "all his actions showed him to be a timorous prince," although he would later prove a good friend to Cook.

Cook had a sad meeting with the mother of Tootaha, "a venerable old lady [who] seized me by both hands and burst into a flood of tears, saying [Tootaha, the friend of Cook, is dead]. I was so much affected by her behavior that it would not have been possible for me to refrain mingling my tears with hers had not Otoo come and snatched me, as it were, from her." Otoo was jealous at Cook's showing friendship for the old woman, but Cook later visited her again to offer presents.

Contrary to Cook's expectations, the Tahitians were not greatly saddened at the news of Tupia's death. Cook thought that the New Zealanders had seemed more concerned for him than the Tahitians. When the ships departed, another young Tahitian went along on the *Resolution*.

Cook returned to two of the neighboring islands that he had stopped at on his first voyage. At Huaheine, the chief, named

Oree, greeted Cook with ceremonial gifts, including five young plantain trees, which were a symbol of peace. Cook had found the Tahitians less prosperous than they had been, but on Huaheine there was an abundance of food. The English traded for a great many hogs, which the islanders seemed happy to exchange.

As the ships departed from Huaheine, the *Adventure* took on its own passenger, a man named Omai, who was destined to charm eighteenth-century London and cause Cook some trouble on his third voyage to the Pacific.

At Raiatea, the next island, Oreo, the chief, came on board the *Resolution* and offered the islanders' strongest token of friendship: He exchanged names with Cook. The chief would in the future be entitled to the name "Toote," which was how the islanders pronounced Cook's name.

Though Cook now had an abundance of hogs, he was offered more at Raiatea and was compelled to take them out of friendship. The *Resolution* departed the island with over 230 hogs, and the *Adventure* with about 150; some of the animals weighed more than a hundred pounds.

While Cook was at Raiatea, the young man from Tahiti found a wife ashore and asked to stay. One of Oreo's young men, named Oedidde, offered to take his place. Cook accepted the offer. Oedidde was to prove popular among the men of the *Resolution*. Clerke, who liked him on sight, wrote that the young man had come aboard because of his desire to see what England was like.

Though Cook continued to be troubled by petty thefts during his stay at the Society Islands, he felt a great affection for the people there: "The more one is acquainted with these people the better one likes them," he wrote. "To give them their due I must say they are the most obliging and benevolent people I ever met with."

His affection was returned. Often the islanders' parting question to Cook was: When would he return? Cook wrote, "My friend Oree of Huaheine was very desirous for me to return to his isle, but as he . . . one time very justly observed that both him and I might be dead, says he, 'Let your sons come. They will be well received.' "

Sailing west, the English ships sighted three small islands on September 23. Cook gave them the name Hervey Islands, after his friend Captain Augustus John Hervey, later Earl of Bristol. They are now grouped with a number of other islands stretching far to the north, bearing the name Cook Islands. Cook had no reason to land there; he was looking for three islands discovered by Tasman in 1643.

On October 2, Cook recognized an island that Tasman had named Middelburg; the islanders called it Eua. This is part of the island group today called Tonga. Unexpectedly, he met with an immense welcome. Rows and rows of canoes swarmed round the ships, with natives inside throwing gifts including whole bolts of cloth into the English ships, and then paddling off without waiting for gifts in exchange.

Cook started for shore in the pinnace, but the welcome was so large he had trouble finding a place to land. The islanders crowded around his boat with cloth, matting, and other gifts. Cook ordered his marines to play their bagpipes, and the native women on the beach sang and danced in return.

Tioonee, the chief of the island, brought Cook and his officers to his house where they watched a native beverage being freshly prepared. Islanders chewed the root of a tree, spit the juice into a container, added water to it and offered it to their guests. Cook wrote, "They made cups of green leaves which held near half a pint and presented to each of us a cup of the liquor, but I was the only one who tasted of it. The manner of brewing had quenched the thirst of everyone else."

Cook sailed on, finding nearby the island called Amsterdam by Tasman, who had reported it held "refreshments in plenty." This was still true 130 years later. Again meeting with a warm reception from the islanders—who called their island Tongatapu—Cook toured the island. Otago, the chief, showed Cook the island's plantations. "I thought I was transported into one of the most fertile plains in Europe," Cook wrote. Numerous islanders traveled back and forth from the plantation to the beach, bringing fruit for a feast.

Cook named the group the Friendly Islands, and would return. Now he sailed south, and by October 21 had New Zealand in sight once again.

The ships made their way toward the anchorage in Queen Charlotte's Sound, but fierce gales blew them off the coast, preventing them from entering Cook Strait. In the storm, the ships became separated. By the time the *Resolution* beat its way back to the coast and into the familiar anchorage of Ship Cove, the *Adventure* was nowhere in sight.

Cook was not alarmed. There was work to be done—repairs to the sails, caulking of the hull, and replacement of some of the ironwork. Cook set up a forge ashore, and waited for the *Adventure* to appear.

On shore, Cook discovered that the Maoris had eaten most of the livestock he had left there earlier. He was disappointed: "Thus all our endeavors for stocking this country with useful animals are likely to be frustrated by the very people whom we meant to serve." Nonetheless he set ashore four more hogs and some chickens. This time, however, he ordered that his men take them inland, leaving them with food that would enable them to survive until they could find their own forage. "This," he wrote, "I did in order to keep them in the woods, lest they should come down to the shore in search of food and be discovered by the natives."

Cook's earlier report of the Maoris' cannibalism had been greeted with disbelief in England. One of the beliefs of the Enlightenment was that mankind in its natural state was innocent and good. Yet new proofs offered themselves. Pickersgill obtained a human head ashore, and brought it to the ship. Cook was absent at the time, and Clerke decided to test one of the Maoris then aboard.

"I asked him," wrote Clerke,

> if he'd eat a piece there directly to which he very cheerfully gave his assent. I then cut a piece off, carried to the fire by his desire, and gave it a little broil upon the grid iron, then delivered it to him. He not only ate it but devoured it most ravenously, and sucked his fingers half a dozen times over in raptures.

The effect on the hard-bitten English seamen was to cause some of them to rush to the rail and vomit.

Cook had not been deceived by the myth of the "noble savage"; neither was he quick to condemn people who seemed barbaric to Europeans. Commenting on Clerke's report in his own journal, he wrote:

> few consider what a savage man is in his original state and even after he is in some degree civilized; the New Zealanders are certainly in a state of civilization. Their behavior to us has been manly and mild, showing always a readiness to oblige us. . . . They are far less addicted to thieving than the other Islanders and are, I believe, strictly honest among themselves.

Cook was anxious to get to sea again. He had only a few months of "good" sailing weather to explore the far southern part of the Pacific. He left a message for Furneaux buried under a tree. He told Furneaux that there was little chance of their meeting again, although he suggested that he might try to be at Easter Island toward the end of the following March.

Though Cook had wanted two ships for the voyage as a safety measure, he had often experienced delays in waiting for the slower-sailing *Adventure* to catch up to the *Resolution*. There was also the problem that Furneaux's laxer discipline created health problems aboard the *Adventure*. His crew was less likely than Cook's to be able to endure the polar weather through which Cook would be sailing for the next three months. In his journal Cook reported that he supposed that Furneaux even then might be on his way back to England; he had no doubt that Furneaux could reach there safely.

Ironically Furneaux did reach Ship Cove only about a week after Cook left. He found Cook's message, and did make his way back to England via Cape Horn. But while at Ship Cove he encountered more horrifying evidence of the cannibalism of the Maoris. Ten of his men were captured ashore, slaughtered, and eaten. Furneaux left without taking reprisals and was back in England by April of the following year. He was hailed as the first commander to circumnavigate the globe from west to east, and his passenger, Omai, was the toast of London.

IV

MEANWHILE, COOK WAS SAILING almost due south, straight into the teeth of the ice. He was to chart a gigantic zigzag path across the South Pacific, first sailing as near the pack ice as he could, then turning north, then back again. It was the most effective way of covering the largest area of the South Pacific, sailing directly over the area in which the Southern Continent had long been thought to exist.

Every time the ship encountered icebergs there was danger of collision. And as the *Resolution* approached the solid sheet of ice far to the south, Cook sailed far more closely than his crew would have liked. A sailing ship does not have the maneuverability of an engine-powered vessel, which can change course whenever it is necessary. Unexpected winds—and here they seemed to blow frequently from the north—might at any time force the *Resolution* against the ice before the sails could be lowered. Seldom was the sea bottom shallow enough for the *Resolution*'s anchor to be used to stop the ship.

Midshipman Elliott, now fifteen years old, described the danger on one occasion:

> While amongst the ice islands, we had the most miraculous escape from being every soul lost, that ever men had; . . . the officer of the watch on deck, while the people were at dinner, had the imprudence to attempt going to windward of an island of ice. . . . He got so near that he could get neither one way nor the other, but appeared inevitably going right upon it, and [the iceberg] was twice as high as our mastheads. . . . Capt. Cook ordered light spars to be got ready to push the ship from the island if she came so near, but had she come within their reach . . . [the shock of collision] would have knocked the ship to pieces and drowned us all. . . . But most providentially for us, she went clear.

Cook himself admitted, "According to the old proverb a miss is as good as a mile, but our situation requires more misses than we can expect."

On December 21, the ship crossed the Antarctic Circle for

the second time. A few days after Christmas, Clerke counted 238 ice islands in the sea around the *Resolution*. Cook gave the crew a Christmas present by turning north. Yet on January 11, having reached latitude 48°S, he reversed his course once again. Elliott recorded the feelings of the crew as the ship turned south:

> At this time we all experienced a very severe mortification, for . . . we had all taken it into our heads that we were going straight for Cape Horn, on our route home, for we began to find that our stock of tea, sugar, etc., began to fade, and many hints were thrown out to Capt. Cook to this effect, but he only smiled and said nothing, for he was close and secret in his intentions at all times, that not even his first lieutenant knew, when we left a place, where we should go next. In this respect, as well as many others, he was the fittest man in the world for such a voyage. In this instance, all our hopes were blasted in a minute, for from steering east, at noon Captain Cook ordered the ship to steer due south, to our utter astonishment, and had the effect for a moment of causing a buzz in the ship, but which soon subsided.

Only a commander like Cook who could discipline with a balance between firmness and humaneness could drive the men forward without protest. The crew by now knew that whatever Cook might ask of them, he kept them miraculously healthy and safe.

Every speck on the sea and in the sky was examined for portents of something—anything but the empty sea. Cook was particularly puzzled at the frequent sight of birds called "divers," or diving petrels. "I should have thought them signs of the vicinity of land, as I never saw any so far from known land before." If a crew member spied even so small a thing as a piece of seaweed floating in the water, it was reported to Cook.

Storms battered the ship, but the *Resolution* held together, though "the sea ran prodigious high" was a typical entry in Cook's journal. Expanded, in Forster's journal, to:

> At nine o'clock a huge mountainous wave struck the ship on the beam and filled the decks with a deluge of water. It poured through the skylight over our heads, and extinguished the candle, leaving us for a moment in doubt whether we were not totally overwhelmed and sinking into the abyss.

On January 26, 1774, the *Resolution* crossed the Antarctic Circle for the third time in the voyage—the only three times the line had ever been crossed by human beings. On the same day, Cook wrote—with no hint of the excitement the sight must have caused on ship—"Saw an appearance of land to the east and SE. Hauled up for it and presently after, it disappeared in the haze. Sounded but found no ground with a line of 130 fathoms." The following day, the fog became so thick that Cook tacked slowly to the east, daring no further passage to the south until the weather cleared.

On January 30, the weather did clear. Soon the *Resolution* turned south again, the eyes of every man aboard turning toward the horizon for sight of land. Through a long night, the ship rode the wind, and then at daybreak, the clouds on the horizon appeared. To Cook, they were of "an unusual snow white brightness which [denoted] our approach to field ice." By eight o'clock that morning the ship had reached the edge of the ice.

It was an immense, apparently limitless plain of ice, extending east, west, and south beyond the horizon. The horizon line itself was a shining bar of white reflecting the sun's rays on the ice. The sight prompted even Cook to a rare moment of lyrical description: "The clouds near the horizon were of a perfect snow whiteness and were difficult to be distinguished from the ice hills whose lofty summits reached the clouds." Had Cook not heard of ships near Greenland sailing behind such ice packs, "I should not have hesitated one moment in declaring it as my opinion that the ice we now see extended in a solid body quite to the pole."

In fact the ice did extend to the pole. It was the Antarctic ice shelf. Cook encountered it at 71°10'S, farther south than humans had ever gone, and in that area (longitude 106°54'W) no ship—to this day—has ever been able to travel as far south as the *Resolution*. Cook could not have known that he was only 120 miles away from the ice-covered land that was the seventh continent.

The discovery of Antarctica itself would have to wait for another explorer. No one would have attempted to press farther south in the kind of ship Cook commanded. He wrote:

I will not say it was impossible anywhere to get in among this ice, but I will assert that the bare attempting of it would be a very dangerous enterprise and what I believe no man in my situation would have thought of. I whose ambition leads me not only farther than any other man has been before me, but as far as I think it possible for man to go, was not sorry at meeting with this interruption,

for it meant that he could now turn north for further exploration elsewhere. He had finished his task here; if there were a continent, it was not the size that had been dreamed of, and it would be incapable of supporting human habitation.

The fog soon descended again, causing Cook to reflect how fortunate he had been to have had clear weather when the

Resolution was approaching the ice. Indeed, for the superstitious, it must have seemed that the polar ice unveiled itself for just that moment, to let Cook know that even he must stop here.

What was there left for Cook to do? He proposed to his officers—and Cook's proposals were more like orders than suggestions—to go north to the tropics again, swing west and look for Quirós's Tierra Austrialia del Espiritu Santo. After the winter season in the Southern Hemisphere had passed, he would sail round Cape Horn and explore the southern part of the Atlantic.

Formally, Cook recorded the reaction to his proposal:

> I should not do my officers justice if I did not take some opportunity to declare that they always showed the utmost readiness to carry into execution . . . every measure I thought proper to take. Under such circumstances it is hardly necessary to say that the seamen were always obedient and alert and on this occasion they were so far from wishing the voyage at an end that they rejoiced at the prospect of its being prolonged another year and soon enjoying the benefits of a milder climate.

If they truly rejoiced at the prospect of being at sea another year, then they were worthy of their captain. Certainly, they must have rejoiced at turning away at last from the frozen waters of the Antarctic.

V

THE MILDER CLIMATE came soon enough. By February 22, the temperature was 69°F. It seemed to benefit all but Cook, who now fell gravely ill. He may have been ill for some time, for we know from Sparrman's account that he set an example for his men of not complaining or showing weakness while on duty. His own journal tells us little about his illness.

Whatever it was, it kept him from digesting his food. The ship's surgeon, knowing that all aboard had been living on rations of salted meat for fourteen weeks, thought that fresh meat might help Cook to keep down a meal. There was only one possible source on board: Forster's dog.

Forster had been vocal in his criticism of Cook, and was by all accounts the most unpopular man on board. Yet he was generous on this occasion, and the dog was butchered and cooked. It may have saved the captain's life. Cook kept up his journal throughout his illness, and maintained his usual habit of dispassionate observation. On the meal of roast dog: "I could eat of this flesh as well as broth made of it when I could taste nothing else. Thus I received nourishment and strength from food which would have made most people in Europe sick." Cook was up and around again in a few days.

On March 11, the lookout on the masthead sighted land. Clearly visible on the beaches were a series of "monuments or idols," as Cook described them. It could only be the strange place that the Dutch sailor Roggeveen had named Easter Island in 1721.

The Dutch author who reported on Roggeveen's voyage had described the place with such a mixture of fantasy and fact that no one had been sure that it actually existed. The Dutch author had described the inhabitants as painted brown and standing twelve feet high; the women were supposed to have been painted red and ten to eleven feet tall. The great stone idols that stood on the beach were described in terms that made them sound equally fantastic.

Cook soon discovered that the people of Easter Island were not much different from the islanders he had met elsewhere.

The first night near the island, an islander in a canoe came aboard the ship at Cook's invitation, and Cook observed him stepping off the length of the ship, counting as he walked. Cook realized that the numbers the man used were the same as those in the language of Tahiti, some three thousand miles away.

Cook again shows unusual perceptiveness in concluding there was a link between these islanders and those as far west as New Zealand. Modern anthropologists speculate in their turn that the people of the Marquesas—Polynesians—at some point in the past were responsible for populating Easter Island.

When Cook went ashore to observe, he saw that the people were tattooed in black, and used red and white paint to mark their faces and bodies. If anything they were shorter than the average Tahitian. Both men and women slit their earlobes and placed rings of increasing size in the holes to stretch the lobes, some to a length of three inches.

The most fantastic feature of the island was, to Cook's astonishment, real. There indeed stood massive stone statues that seemed as remarkable as any monument in Europe. The figures, which with their long earlobes seemed to represent effigies of islander faces, stood on foundation squares twenty to thirty feet on a side and ten to twelve feet high. On top of these, the gray stone statues ranged another fifteen to thirty feet in height. Most of the faces were topped by circular red stones, resembling caps; an average red stone was fifty-two inches high and sixty-six inches in diameter.

Cook observed that the statues marked family burial places, like the *maraes* of Polynesia. He would not be the last, however, to puzzle over the origin of the effigies, which has never been completely explained: "We could hardly conceive how a nation like these, wholly unacquainted with every mechanical power, could raise such stupendous figures and afterwards place the large cylindric stones . . . upon their heads."

The ship's artist, William Hodges, made paintings of the huge effigies, leaving a valuable historical record. In the succeeding years, battles among the islanders resulted in the toppling of many of the idols, and European missionaries in the next century ordered the destruction of many more. Few today stand as Cook and his men saw them.

Cook had no time to solve the mystery of the Easter Island effigies. There was not sufficient food or water on the island to supply the *Resolution*, and by the sixteenth of March, Cook had set sail again.

Somewhere to the west of here, Cook calculated, were the islands called the Marquesas, first visited in 1595 by Mendaña. Using Mendaña's vague accounts and his own knowledge of the Pacific, Cook rediscovered the Marquesas on April 6, identifying them from the description in the account of Mendaña's second voyage.

Cook's usual restrictions on trade broke down when the Marquesans found that the ship had red feathers aboard. The red feathers, which Cook had obtained on Tonga, were much in demand among the Pacific islands that had no birds with red plumage. The Marquesans would accept only red feathers for their trade goods, and, Cook wrote, "our market was at once spoiled and I was obliged to return [to the ship] with three or four little pigs which cost me more than a dozen would have the evening before."

On the twelfth of April, Cook ordered the *Resolution* put to sea again, on a course that he knew would take him to Tahiti if no other islands lay in between. He did in fact sight two other islands, first discovered by Roggeveen and then again by Byron, who named them King George's Islands. They were of no particular importance, except that Cook now realized that by calculating their position—as he accurately computed it with the help of the watches—he could determine more accurately where the rest of Byron's discoveries lay. He would later adjust Bougainville's map in the same way when he reached one of the islands the Frenchman had reached, but charted only approximately.

On April 22 the *Resolution* anchored off Tahiti in the now-familiar Matavai Bay. Otoo, the "king," came on board with his followers to welcome Cook. He brought a dozen hogs, and the officers and chiefs enjoyed a sumptuous feast.

Cook established a regular trade, this time governing the trade of red feathers, which he found were also in great demand here. He observed that the islanders were more prosperous than when he had seen them last, and decided the island could support his crew long enough for repairs on the ship. The crew settled in for a well-deserved rest. The red feathers that each man had collected would bring the luxuries of a paradise.

On the morning of the twenty-sixth, Cook set out with the Forsters and some of his officers to return Otoo's visit. They found a rare sight awaiting them near the shore—some three hundred war canoes, completely equipped and manned, ranged in ceremonial order for Cook's review. "Canoe," as we use the word, hardly seems sufficient to describe the Tahitians' war craft. The larger boats, of which there were 160, could each contain some 40 rowers and warriors. The smaller canoes, equipped with sails, carried about eight crew members, but were large enough to carry cargo or those wounded in battle.

The chiefs on the large canoes wore turbans, breast plates, and helmets, which Cook thought must be for ceremony, for they were of such length and design as to be impractical in battle. Later he learned otherwise: The display was part of the attack, intended to frighten the foe. The boats were decorated with flags, streamers, and paint, "so that," Cook wrote, "the whole made a grand and noble appearance such as was never seen before in this sea."

As Cook admiringly inspected the naval display, he became conscious that he was now a figure in an island rivalry which he little understood. The islanders on shore began to chant "Tiyo no Otoo," which Cook knew referred to him as "friend of Otoo." At the same time the men in the boats began to chant, "Tiyo no Towha." Towha, the admiral of the fleet, now made his appearance and urged Cook to continue his inspection of the boats. Before Cook could reply, they were joined by Tee, the uncle of Otoo, who insisted that Cook must first come ashore for Otoo's greeting.

Clearly, the dispute was a point of prestige between Otoo and Towha. Tee had hold of one of Cook's hands, Towha the other, and they were pulling in opposite directions. "Between the one party and the other, I was like to have been torn to pieces," Cook recalled, and he decided to compromise by remaining in his own boat until Otoo should arrive.

Otoo, however, was nowhere to be found. Unknown to Cook, the chief had just heard the news that one of the islanders had stolen some of Cook's clothes from the washing place farther inland.

Towha finally gave up the struggle and departed, clearly offended. Cook was disappointed, because

I lost the opportunity of examining more narrowly into a part of the naval force of this island and making myself better acquainted how it acts and is conducted. Such opportunity may never happen again, as it was commanded by a brave, sensible, and intelligent chief who no doubt would have satisfied us in all the questions we had thought proper to ask.

Before long, Cook was able to make up the differences between him and the two chiefs. He found Otoo, who told Cook that he was *mata-ou,* which meant embarrassed over the theft but also carried the meaning of being "in hiding." In the days that followed, Cook learned that the occurrence of a theft was quickly signaled by the disappearance of most of the islanders from the trading area. They too went into *mata-ou* until Cook's intentions to punish or forgive became known.

Cook's punishments, normally the seizure of boats or some other property until the stolen objects were returned, were backed up by the Tahitians' knowledge of the power of English firearms. Otoo, seeking to enhance his own prestige as Cook's friend, asked the captain for a public demonstration of English power. Cook's marines complied with a drill in which they demonstrated the use of the muskets. The ship's guns were called on to fire a ceremonial salute, and Cook ordered an evening display of fireworks.

The islanders were seemingly impressed, but the petty thievery continued, and Cook struggled—as he did with his own men—to find the correct line between discipline and leniency. Cook concluded that three things kept the peaceful relationship between his men and the islanders. First was the Tahitians' "good-natured and benevolent disposition." Second was "gentle treatment on our part." Third was the islanders' dread of firearms. But, Cook added,

> by our ceasing to observe the second, the first would have worn off . . . , and the too frequent use of [the third] would have excited a spirit of revenge and perhaps have taught them that firearms were not such terrible things as they had imagined. They are very sensible of the superiority they have over us in numbers and no one knows what an enraged multitude might do.

By May 13, repairs to the *Resolution* were complete, and Cook made plans to sail. To Cook's relief, both Towha and Otoo came aboard to make their farewells. Towha was ailing, and his feet were swollen. Cook had him hoisted aboard the ship and placed in a chair. Cook gave the two chiefs a number of gifts, but the one that pleased "admiral" Towha most was an officer's pennant of the British navy, for him to display on his canoe.

Not to be outdone by the display of canoes that Towha had again prepared, Otoo had his fighting men give a display of their skills with clubs and spears. In fighting with the clubs, Cook observed that "all side-blows were parried with the club except those intended for the legs, which were evaded by leaping over them. A downright blow on the head they evaded by crouching a little and leaping on one side." Their methods of defending against attack by spears were even more spectacular: "They parried off the spear or dart by fixing the point of [their own] spear in the ground," and by moving it to the left or right deflected thrown spears, a display of amazing dexterity.

There was one more adventure before Cook could depart from Tahiti. In the confusion of the ceremonies, a gunner's mate named John Marra slipped overboard and tried to swim ashore. He was soon noticed, and a boat picked him out of the water.

Surprisingly, Marra's punishment was very lenient; Cook merely ordered him kept in irons until the ship was well away from the island. Cook confided the reasons for his lenience to his journal, betraying his own wistful feelings at the departure. He pointed out that Marra had served on both this voyage and the preceding one as a good sailor. Marra had no relatives or close friends in England, and "all nations were alike to him. Where then can such a man spend his days better than at one of these isles where he can enjoy all the necessaries and some of the luxuries of life in ease and plenty?"

Cook even mused, "I know not if [Marra] might not have obtained my consent [to stay in Tahiti] if he had applied for it in proper time." That was really a remarkable statement for a man in Cook's position, considering that there must have been many aboard who had entertained the same thoughts as Marra.

On May 24, the ship reached the harbor at the south end of Raiatea. Oreo, the chief of the island, came out bringing gifts even before Cook had anchored. Cook and his officers were treated to a banquet ashore. The Raiateans entertained them with plays—in which the Englishmen perceived that they were sometimes impersonated by the actors, though their scanty command of the language kept them from understanding their lines. In one play, a bearded man impersonated a woman giving birth; a cloth was laid over him and another actor crawled under the cloth to portray the newborn baby coming forth: "a thumping boy near six feet high," Cook recounted. He noted that some of the others held the "newborn" and pressed his nose flat, which led Cook to conclude that it was an imitation of an actual birth ceremony that might account for the fact that all the Raiateans had pug noses.

Oedidde was now at his home island, and Cook expected to leave him there. However, Oreo continually pressed Cook to say he would return someday, and whenever Cook out of politeness indicated that this might be possible, Oedidde began to talk excitedly of traveling with Cook to England and returning on the next voyage.

Finally, Cook made it clear to Oreo that he could never return. Disappointed, the chief asked Cook the name of his *marae*, the island name for burial place. "A strange question to ask a seaman," Cook commented, who was aware of his chances for a watery grave, but "I hesitated not one moment to tell him Stepney, the parish in which I lived when in London." The islanders asked him to repeat the name until they could pronounce it, and then the phrase "Stepney Marae no Totee" (Stepney is the burial place of Cook) "was echoed through a hundred mouths at once." It must have had an eerie sound, even for Cook, a man who never seems to have doubted that his destiny and ambition would overcome the risks he ran at sea.

Oedidde stayed with the ship until the last moment, still torn as to where his own destiny would take him. He asked Cook to *tattaow* some *parou*, or mark some words, for him, and Cook "complied . . . by giving him a certificate of his good behavior, the time . . . he had been with us, and recommended him to the notice of those who might come to these isles after me." When Oedidde finally left, Cook wrote, "I have not words to describe the anguish which appeared in this young man's breast when he went away; he looked up at the ship, burst into tears, and then sunk down into the canoe."

Cook sailed west, adding new islands to his chart. At Tonga, or the Friendly Islands, Cook rediscovered the third of the islands Tasman had visited in 1643. Islanders there gave Cook a chart of some twenty other islands in the group.

By the accounts of all those who sailed with him, Cook never gave in to the temptations offered by the islanders' casual attitude toward sex. At Nomuka, one of the Friendly Islands, his chastity and pride got a severe test. An old woman brought him an attractive young woman "and gave me to understand she was at my service." Cook wrote with wry humor of the exchange that followed:

Miss [as he called the younger woman] wanted . . . a shirt or a nail. Neither the one nor the other I had to give without giving her the shirt on my back, which I was not in a humor to do. I soon made them sensible of my poverty and thought by that means to have come off with flying colors, but I was mistaken, for I was made to understand I might retire with her on credit. This not suiting me neither, the old lady began first to argue with me and when that failed she abused me. I understood very little of what she said, but her actions were expressive enough and showed that her words were to this effect . . . what sort of a man are you thus to refuse the embraces of so fine a young woman, for the girl certainly did not [want] beauty, which I could however withstand, but the abuse of the old woman I could not and therefore hastened into the boat.

Continuing to sail west, Cook touched on Vatoa, one of the group today known as Fiji, but he remained ignorant of the larger islands in the group, which lay to the north. By the seventeenth of July he was in sight of an island that he recognized as one that Bougainville had called Aurora Island. Bougainville's charts showed it twenty miles to the north of its true position, a judgment Cook could now make with certainty.

Cook was now in the islands known today as the New Hebrides. He came to an anchorage at the island of Malekula. He deduced, correctly, that he was in the group of islands called Austrialia del Espiritu Santo by Quirós. It was late in the day; by the setting sun, the men of the *Resolution* could see islanders ashore armed with bows and arrows, held in ready positions.

After the sun set, canoes came out to the now-anchored ship. The islanders bore no resemblance to the Polynesians of Tahiti and Tonga; these people were part of Melanesia. Cook wrote that "they are the most ugly and ill-proportioned people I ever saw and in every respect different from any we had yet seen in this sea."

Cook persuaded the men in the canoes to come aboard: "The kind reception these met with induced others to come off by moonlight . . . they exchanged for pieces of cloth some few arrows, some of which were pointed with bone and dipped in poison or some green gummy substance that could answer to no other end."

The following morning, more canoes lay alongside the ship, and Cook invited the new visitors to come on board. He led some of them to his cabin, which had a window in the stern of the ship. Through the window came the sounds of an argument. Another islander was attempting to make off with one of the *Resolution*'s small boats. When the boatkeeper waved him off, the islander began to string his bow.

Immediately, one of the islanders inside Cook's cabin jumped through the window and began to struggle with the thief. Cook recounted that the thief

> got the better of him and directed his bow again to the boat keeper, but upon my calling to him he directed it to me and was just going to let fly when I gave him a peppering of small shot [from his musket]. This staggered him for a moment but did not hinder him from holding his bow in the attitude of shooting. Another discharge . . . made him drop it and the others in the canoes to paddle off as fast as they could.

The islanders whom Cook had befriended quickly left the ship, and Cook resolved to go ashore. Facing "about 400 or 500 men who were assembled on the shore, armed with bows and arrows, clubs and spears," Cook took a small boat ashore with a few officers and men.

As Cook's boat neared the beach, a man came out alone in a canoe. He left his weapons ashore and offered a green branch to Cook. When they reached the shore, the man led Cook up the beach by the hand. The captain distributed medals, cloth, and other presents, and through sign language indicated that he wanted to cut some wood. The islanders seemed to give their approval, and brought out a small pig as a present for Cook.

He showed that he wished to trade for more pigs, but the

islanders only offered some coconuts. Unlike the Polynesians, the people here "set no sort of value upon nails, nor did they seem much to esteem anything we had," Cook wrote. "They would now and then give an arrow for a piece of cloth, but constantly refused to part with their bows." Nonetheless, Cook noted, the islanders were scrupulously honest after the first incident.

The *Resolution* continued on through the New Hebrides, finding that in some places the offer of a green branch guaranteed peace. In other places, Cook ordered his men to withdraw in the face of unmistakable hostility.

Cook was tolerant of the islanders' distrust. He wrote:

We found these people civil and good-natured when not prompted by jealousy to a contrary conduct, a conduct one cannot blame them for when one considers the light in which they must look upon us. It is impossible for them to know our real design. We enter their ports without their daring to make opposition. We attempt to land in a peaceable manner. If this succeeds, it's well; if not we land nevertheless and maintain the footing . . . by the superiority of our firearms. In what other light can they then at first look upon us but as invaders of their country. Time and some acquaintance with us can only convince them of their mistake.

The people in these islands were obviously of a different culture from those Cook had visited to the east. Forster wanted to stop for a time to observe them. Cook landed at the island of Tanna, and found that the islanders demanded that any Englishmen coming to their homes strip "naked as they were." He and Forster complied. The men on Tanna wore only a leaf; the English settled for underwear.

There was an active volcano on the island of Tanna. In the night it threw up vast quantities of fire and smoke, and made a noise that sounded to Cook like "thunder or the blowing up of mines at every eruption, which happened every four or five minutes; a heavy shower of rain which fell at this time seemed to increase it." Fine ash covered everything on board the *Resolution*; the men found that it stung their eyes constantly.

Forster and Cook tried to persuade some islanders to take them to the mouth of the volcano. The islanders, who must have thought the request strange, obligingly led them on an all-day wild goose chase that wound about the interior, never getting near the volcano, until they emerged again onto the beach.

Wales, the astronomer, pursued his own studies of the island culture. He was so impressed by the people of Tanna that he likened them to the heroes of Homeric epics. Wales confessed that he had thought the feats of mythical Greeks described by Homer were fantasy, until he had seen the islanders fling a spear sixty to seventy yards with fair accuracy.

Cook knew that the islands to the north had been called Santa Cruz by Quirós; they seemed the same as those sighted by Carteret in 1767. There seemed no point in going to confirm that discovery, so he now turned south, heading for New Zealand.

There were other discoveries to be made before he arrived in the familiar Queen Charlotte's Sound. On September 4, the lookout on the *Resolution* sighted land at eight in the morning. By noon the land filled the horizon, and it was still six leagues ahead. This was no tiny atoll; it was the largest land mass in the South Pacific aside from the islands of New Zealand; Cook would call it New Caledonia.

The people of New Caledonia proved to be friendly, though their standard of living was below that of the Polynesians.

Coming aboard the *Resolution*, some of them remarked with surprise at the animals aboard. They had no previous knowledge of goats, dogs, cats, or hogs.

Cook saw an opportunity to accomplish one of his personal aims: to enrich the islands by introducing new kinds of animals and plants that the islanders would find useful. He brought ashore a boar and a sow and had his men carry them to the chief's residence. Cook gives a sidelight on his own trading skills. Inside the hut there were eight to ten middle-aged men

> to whom I and my pigs were introduced and with great courtesy I was desired to sit down. I began to expatiate on the merits of the two pigs, showing them the distinction of their sex, telling them how many young ones the female would have at a time. In short I multiplied them to some hundreds in a trice. My only view was to enhance the value of the present that they might take the more care of them, and I had reasons to think I in some measure succeeded.

Cook attempted to sail northwest around the island, but dangerous shoals like those that nearly wrecked his first ship, the *Endeavour*, made him turn in the other direction. At the southeast end of New Caledonia, he sighted several small islands that held a startling sight—something that at first looked like a fleet of ships at anchor, their bare masts rising high in the air.

There were many opinions aboard ship as to the nature of the odd formation. Forster, the trained scientist, thought they were stone pillars, natural formations like the basaltic columns of Ireland that are known as the Giant's Causeway. Cook disagreed; he thought they were "a singular sort of tree, being too numerous to be anything else."

The *Resolution* was not able to get close enough for a better view of the island. In a few days, another island with the same odd formations appeared. Cook called it the Isle of Pines, against the protests of Forster, who argued that the formations were too high and too straight to be trees. The tricky winds and shoals along the coast made sailing increasingly dangerous. When Cook rounded the tip of New Caledonia, he found that the winds and tides made it almost impossible to continue along the south coast.

Cook wrote, "I was now almost tired of a coast I could no longer explore [except] at the risk of losing the ship . . . but I was determined not to leave it till I was satisfied what sort of trees those were which had been the subject of our speculation."

Cook's curiosity had a strictly practical side. He knew that if in fact the tall formations were trees, they could be an important resource for a ship in these waters in need of masts. The *Resolution* itself had used its supply of replacement cross-spars. As Cook attempted to draw closer, however, the danger grew so great that the *Resolution* spent one long night "making short boards," tacking frequently to keep from being dashed against the rocky coast. During that night, each man on duty never let go of the rope to which he was assigned so that the sails could be shifted as soon as the command was given.

Finally, on September 29, the ship came to an anchorage, and Cook and the Forsters went ashore. As Cook had surmised, the formations were indeed trees, what Cook called "a kind of spruce pine." They were giant conifers today known as *Araucaria columnaris* or *Araucaria cooki.* They can grow one hundred feet high, with branches seldom over six feet long, so that knotholes were a minor problem. The wood inside was white, close-grained and tough—ideal for masts.

Cook brought his carpenters ashore to cut some of the trees. An unexpected bonus was the conifers' sticky sap; when mixed with coral sand, it made an excellent substitute for the caulking compound needed to seal the ship's hull. Cook set his men to caulking leaks in the ship as he set his course south for New Zealand.

Midway between New Caledonia and New Zealand, in an otherwise empty sea, Cook sighted another island—one of the few he had found that was uninhabited. Cook called it Norfolk Island, and was agreeably surprised that the trees here were even taller than those on the Isle of Pines. This variety is known as *Araucaria excelsa*. Under the name Norfolk Island Pine, seedlings are sold today as house plants. They grow with such vigor that they can survive in the unfavorable conditions of the average home, though never grow to normal size.

By the middle of October, Cook was back inside Ship Cove in Queen Charlotte's Sound. He looked for the bottle in which he had left a message eleven months before. It was gone, but whoever had taken it had not left his name. It was a puzzle, but more mystifying to Cook was the behavior of the Maoris. Though he was convinced they knew him as a friend, all had fled at the sight of the ship.

Cook was not to learn till much later that Captain Furneaux in the *Adventure* had returned to this spot ten months earlier and that ten of his men had been killed by the Maoris.

The Maoris naturally assumed Cook had come to take vengeance. Before long, he found some of them hiding in the forest, and when they realized he knew nothing of the earlier incident, the rest "hurried out of the woods, embraced us over and over, and skipped about like mad men."

Although Cook at first could find no trace of the animals he had left earlier, or the people to whom he had given them, he was cheered when one of the crew found a freshly laid hen's egg ashore. The following day the Forsters spotted one of the hogs foraging in the forest. Cook reflected with satisfaction that the benefits he thought to bring to these people showed some signs of taking hold.

VI

ON THE MORNING OF NOVEMBER 10, the *Resolution* left New Zealand. Cook resolved to sail in a high latitude straight across the Pacific toward the tip of South America. He would cross directly over what had for centuries been presumed to be the great Southern Continent.

Weather and winds were good, but there were disquieting signs. Not many days' sail from New Zealand, the ship began to take on water forward. The leak was found to be above the water line, but as the ship pitched forward, water gushed into the hold. By now the pine sap from the Isle of Pines had run out, and the carpenters plugged the leak with a mix of cooking fat and chalk. A few days later, one of the sails split and blew apart, and a squall broke one of the masts. Clearly the ship was feeling the ravages of the long voyage. A more cautious captain would have set a course for home as soon as possible.

Cook had other plans. Not only did he intend to finish the voyage with a search of the far South Atlantic for signs of a greatly reduced Southern Continent, but he decided to examine and chart as much of the area around Cape Horn as he could.

On December 17, the men of the *Resolution* sighted the coast of South America. Cook made his way south along the coast, passing a place he called Cape Desolation

because near it commenced the most desolate and barren country I ever saw . . . it seems to be entirely composed

of rocky mountains without the least appearance of vege-
tation. These mountains terminate in horrible precipices
whose craggy summits spire up to a vast height, so that
hardly anything in nature can appear with a more barren
and savage aspect than the whole of this coast.

Despite the danger, Cook risked a landing, bringing the ship
to harbor by using boats to pull her between shoals. Exploration revealed that the cove in which the *Resolution* anchored
had a small stony beach that led to a tree-covered valley,
through which ran a small stream of fresh water. It was ideal
for Cook's purposes, and during the next few days while the
crew brought supplies to the ship, Cook and the scientists traveled to nearby islands in the cutter.

There were hundreds of geese in the area; it was their
moulting season and none of them could fly. Cook reported
that his party bagged sixty-two of them, giving a good Christmas Eve dinner to all aboard ship.

The people in the area were peaceful, and their knives were
of European origin. Either they had seen Europeans before, or
traded with another group who had. Oddly, they were one of
the few peoples Cook encountered to whom he took a dislike.
He called them "a little, ugly, half-starved beardless race; I saw
not a tall person among them. They were almost naked; their
clothing was a seal skin. . . . In the canoes were two women
nursing children who were naked despite the cold weather."
The children seemed not to feel the cold, and Cook concluded
they were inured to it from infancy. Even so, there was a fire in
each canoe "over which the poor creatures huddled."

Perhaps a clue to Cook's disapproval lay in the fact that
these people failed to take advantage of the natural resources
available to them. Cook pointed out that the natives traded
sealskins freely, indicating that they knew how to get more.
Why then did they not provide better garments for themselves?

Cook suggested in his journal that "they might line their seal skin cloaks with the skins and feathers of aquatic birds."

On December 28 the ship set out again. Cook decided to try to chart the precise location of the Dutch discovery of Staten Landt, once thought to be the easternmost point of *Terra Australis*, or the Southern Continent. He reached it on the thirty-first.

Tricky currents made landing dangerous for the ship, and the *Resolution* anchored a mile offshore. Cook sent boats to catch some of the many seals and birds he sighted on shore with his spyglass. The "seals" proved to be seallike animals that the crew called "lions on account of the great resemblance the male has to a land lion. . . . They were all so tame, or rather so stupid, as to suffer us to come so near as to knock them down with a stick, but the large ones we shot as it was rather dangerous to go near them." Some of the males weighed nearly a thousand pounds.

Cook's description of the abundance of seals, sea lions, and later, whales in these waters was to encourage future expeditions to come hunting them for their pelts and blubber. In the early part of the next century, some of these hunters would be the first to sight the continent of Antarctica, from which a peninsula juts out toward South America to within seven hundred miles of Cook's position.

On January 3, 1775, the *Resolution* rounded Staten Landt and returned to the Atlantic. Cook continued to search for some of the real and imagined discoveries that were said to mark a southern continent. On January 14, the lookout sighted something. At first it was thought to be an iceberg, but as the ship drew nearer, it appeared to be land, although completely covered with snow.

The discovery was Willis Island, one of a group of small islands lying off the northeast tip of a much larger island. The large island Cook named South Georgia, after his sovereign,

George III. ("North" Georgia was the colony that would soon become one of the thirteen rebellious states of North America.)

Cook landed at a spot called Possession Bay to take formal possession of the land for the King. He was astonished at the frozen waste that lay before him, in a relatively low latitude (fourteen hundred miles north of the Antarctic Circle) in midsummer. Glaciers extended out from the land in several places. High, sheer cliffs of ice rose up from parts of the coast. Cook observed huge chunks of ice break off from the cliffs and fall into the sea, echoing off the ice cliffs with a noise like cannon firing. He wrote, "The inner parts of the country [were] not less savage and horrible: the wild rocks raised their lofty summits till they were lost in the clouds and the valleys laid buried in everlasting snow. Not a tree or a shrub was to be seen, no not even big enough to make a toothpick."

He was to see an even more barren land. After sailing round South Georgia, determining that it was not part of a continent, but an island, he went southeast and then south, looking again for the rumored Cape Circumcision. By the twenty-seventh he was in the latitude of 60°S once more, and on the following day, "we fell in all at once with a vast number of large ice islands, and a sea strewed with loose ice."

On January 31, the lookout sighted land. It proved to be three ice-choked, rocky islets of considerable height. "Every port," Cook wrote, "was blocked or filled up with ice, and the whole country, from the summits of the mountains down to the very brink of the cliffs which terminate the coast, was covered many fathoms thick with everlasting snow." Along with two other islands nearby the group was named Sandwich Land; on his third voyage, when Cook gave the name Sandwich Islands to Hawaii, these lonely islands in the Atlantic became known as the South Sandwich Islands.

The presence of so many icebergs could not be accounted for by small islands such as South Georgia and the South Sandwich Islands. Yet, Cook reasoned, since the icebergs were made of fresh water, they must have been formed on land. Any such land mass that was left undiscovered must be too near the South Pole to be accessible by ship. In any case, it could offer no hope of natural resources to be exploited. "I can be bold to say," Cook wrote, "that no man will ever venture farther than I have done and that the lands which may lie to the south will never be explored."

Cook enumerated the dangers: thick fogs, snowstorms, intense cold, "the inexpressibly horrid aspect of the country, a country doomed by nature never once to feel the warmth of the sun's rays, but to lie forever buried under everlasting snow and ice." Even if a ship could force its way in, "she runs a risk of being fixed there forever, or coming out in an ice island."

By February 21, Cook was within two degrees of longitude from the place where he had been after leaving the Cape of Good Hope more than two years earlier. Cook felt, finally, that his instructions had been carried out, and he summarized the results of the voyage:

I had now made the circuit of the Southern Ocean in a high latitude and traversed it in such a manner as to leave not the least room for the possibility of there being such a continent, unless near the pole and out of the reach of navigation. By twice visiting the Pacific Tropical Sea, I had not only settled the situation of some old discoveries but made there many new ones and left, I conceive, very little more to be done even in that part. Thus I flatter myself that the intention of the voyage has in every respect been fully answered, the Southern Hemisphere sufficiently explored, and a final end put to the searching after a Southern Continent, which has at times engrossed the attention of some of the maritime powers for near two centuries past and the geographers of all ages.

It was a sweeping statement, almost an arrogant one, for a man with little formal education. Yet it has stood the test of time as pretty nearly accurate; never again would the myth of the Southern Continent be seriously raised. Cook would find on his third voyage that there was more to the Pacific than he had yet found, but when he had finished there would be little left for explorers except to fill in details on his maps. His most remarkable achievement was to locate the scattered islands with such precision that future sailors could return to them without difficulty.

Cook realized it was time to go home. His people were still healthy "and could cheerfully have gone wherever I had thought proper to lead them," but the supplies of antiscorbutics were beginning to run out; without them he could not hope to continue evading scurvy for long. By the eighth of March, the *Resolution* had seen the last of the ice islands, and the temperature was a balmy 61°F. Cook and his men put away their heavy clothes for the last time.

On March 18, the ship met several other vessels that had recently left the Cape of Good Hope. On one, there were English sailors who sent a message to Cook reporting that the *Adventure* had reached the Cape twelve months before, and that one of her boat's crews had been murdered by cannibals on New Zealand.

In his journal Cook resolved to make "no reflections on this melancholy affair until I hear more about it. I must, however, observe in favor of the New Zealanders that I have always found them of a brave, noble, open and benevolent disposition, but they are a people that will never put up with an insult if they have the opportunity to resent it."

The British ship also sent Cook fresh provisions, tea, and a parcel of old newspapers, which the men of the *Resolution* pored over, trying to acquaint themselves with three years of history that they had missed, and perhaps to find the old news of the death of a friend or relative.

Among the most surprising bits of news to a crew that had not been in contact with Europe since 1772 was that the thirteen colonies of North America had united in revolt against British rule. Amazingly, these brash colonials had already won a few minor battles against British troops.

In Cook's log it was March 21 when he anchored in Cape Town, where it was March 22—the *Resolution* had gained a day circumnavigating the globe in an easterly direction. The *Resolution*, Cook calculated, had come "no less than 20,000 leagues [63,600 nautical miles, or about 73,000 miles on land], a distance I will be bold to say was never sailed by any ship in the same space of time before."

On April 27, the *Resolution* was judged shipshape and put to sea once more. On May 15 the ship put in at the familiar port of St. Helena, in the Atlantic Ocean. At Cape Town, Cook had been mortified to read the garbled version of his first journal that had been prepared by the English man of letters, Dr. Hawkesworth. It contained, among many errors, a derogatory account of the residents of St. Helena that bore no resemblance to Cook's original writings. After necessary apologies to his hosts, he resolved there not to allow another such butchering of his second journal.

Remarkably, Cook was not through with discoveries. After putting in at the island of Ascension, to gather turtle meat, he sailed across the Atlantic again, headed for the island of Fernando de Noronha off the coast of Brazil. Cook was now aware that the still-functioning copy of Harrison's timepiece enabled him to determine the location of any spot in the world with greater accuracy than any previous method. He wanted to mark the location of the island, very near to the easternmost point of South America, and was unwilling "to give up every object which might tend to the improvement of navigation and geography for the sake of getting home a week or a fortnight sooner." Thus the trip across the Atlantic, which had been almost unthinkable at the time of Columbus less than three centuries earlier, was only a minor detour for the man who had mapped the Pacific.

Finally the crew breathed a collective sigh of relief on July 29 when the *Resolution* made the land near Plymouth, England, and anchored at Spithead the next morning. Cook's second journal ends with the words, "Having been absent from England three years and eighteen days, in which time I lost but four men and only one of them by sickness."

CHAPTER FOUR

Resolution AND Discovery, 1776-1780

I

FASTER SHIPS from the Cape of Good Hope had already reported to the Admiralty the news of Cook's success. When Cook arrived, he was greeted as a hero. He was given a promotion to post-captain and offered the position of captain of the Royal Hospital at Greenwich, which was governed by the navy. The position was a sinecure—there were few real duties, and the salary for the post would allow Cook and his family to live comfortably for the rest of their lives.

Cook accepted his new assignment with one condition: that the Lords of the Admiralty "will allow me to quit it when . . . the call of my country for more active service . . . can be essential to the public." Privately, in a letter to his old friend and employer John Walker, he said, "My fate drives me from one extreme to another. A few months ago the whole Southern Hemisphere was hardly big enough for me and now I am going to be confined within the limits of Greenwich Hospital, which are far too small for an active mind like

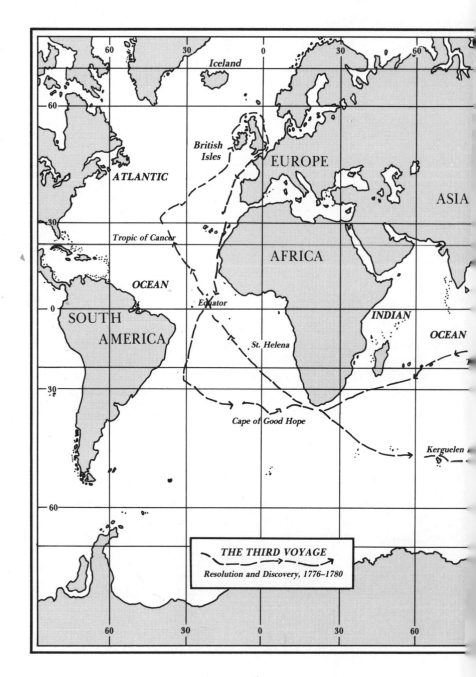

Iceland

60

British
Isles

EUROPE

ASIA

ATLANTIC

Tropic of Cancer

AFRICA

OCEAN

Equator

SOUTH
AMERICA

INDIAN

St. Helena

OCEAN

Cape of Good Hope

Kerguelen

THE THIRD VOYAGE
Resolution and Discovery, 1776–1780

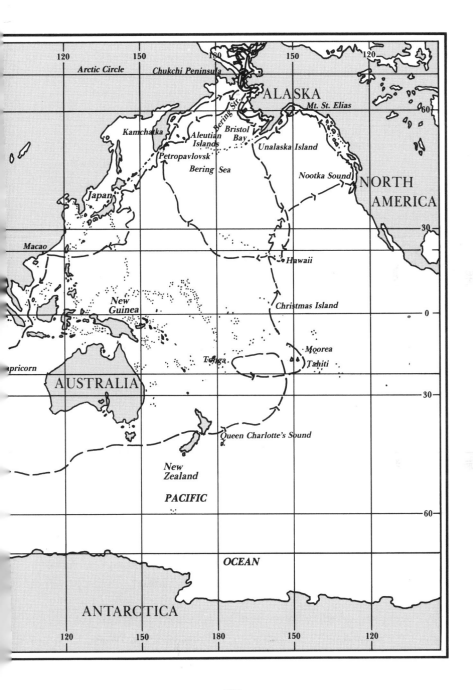

Arctic Circle Chukchi Peninsula

ALASKA

Mt. St. Elias

Kamchatka Bristol
Aleutian Bay
Islands Unalaska Island

Petropavlovsk

Bering Sea Nootka Sound

Japan NORTH
AMERICA

Macao

Hawaii

New
Guinea Christmas Island

Moorea
Tonga Tahiti

AUSTRALIA

New
Zealand Queen Charlotte's Sound

PACIFIC

OCEAN

ANTARCTICA

137

mine . . . whether I can bring myself to like ease and retirement, time will show."

Already the Admiralty was planning another voyage to the Pacific. The *Resolution* was sent to Deptford shipyard for refitting, and Clerke placed in command. The announced reason for the proposed voyage was to return Omai to his people.

When Captain Furneaux and the *Adventure* had returned to England, Omai, the islander from Huaheine, had become something of a celebrity. English society, which thought itself sophisticated in the principles of science, embraced Omai as the representative of "natural man." His portrait was painted, he was invited to social and intellectual gatherings, and was the subject of articles and verses in the popular newspapers. His hosts wanted to hear his comments on England and its manners and customs.

Cook continued to resist becoming engulfed by invitations from those who wished to exhibit *him* on their guest list. The abashed Banks made congratulations to Cook and commissioned an artist, Nathaniel Dance, to paint Cook's portrait. Cook "spared a few hours" for the sitting, and the result was the most famous portrait of Cook, showing a powerful, intense man seated with his finger on a chart and turning as if to make a deeply important statement about his discoveries. It caught the power and dignity of the man, but perhaps not the openness that had allowed him to make friends with the many peoples of the Pacific.

Cook was now engrossed with editing his own journal of the second voyage. When he met the famous biographer James Boswell, he complained about the hash that Hawkesworth had made of his first journal. Boswell remarked, "Why, Sir, Hawkesworth has used your narrative as a London tavern-keeper does wine. He has brewed it." Cook had no wish for his second journal to be brewed in such a fashion, and he worked long and hard to prepare it for suitable publication in his own words. Eventually he collaborated with another literary executor, who produced a version that was more Cook than fantasy. Even so, Cook's own journals, published as he wrote them on ship, were not printed until 1955. They are judged more powerful without the cultured rewriting that they were subjected to in Cook's lifetime.

Cook kept in touch with the plans for another Pacific voyage. Clerke required a second ship for the return trip; Cook helped select it. In the meantime the Lords of the Admiralty began to plan a grander purpose for the voyage than merely returning Omai to his people. They were considering it as part of an effort to discover the long-sought Northwest Passage.

Columbus sailed in 1492 expecting to cross the Atlantic Ocean to reach the spice-rich Indies. His discovery that another continent lay in between enlarged human knowledge of the geography of the world. Yet the search for a sea route to the Indies continued.

The Spanish eventually reached the Indies by sailing south and west around the southern tip of South America. The Portuguese reached the Indies by sailing around the southern part of Africa and going east.

As early as 1527, an Englishman, Robert Thorne, noted that "there is one way [left] to discover, which is into the North." For well into the nineteenth century, explorers were to search for the Northwest Passage. In 1576 Sir Martin Frobisher reached the interior of the Hudson Strait before returning. In 1610 Henry Hudson passed through this strait into the bay that bears his name. But at James Bay his crew mutinied, leaving Hudson and his young son to freeze. Later voyagers continued to search Hudson Bay, without success, for an outlet that would take them to the Pacific.

In 1616 William Baffin sailed up the west coast of Greenland to the head of what is today known as Baffin Bay. He reached latitude 78°N, and on his return trip down the western shore of the bay found three outlets to the west. He failed to recognize these as channels, however, and his discoveries were lost to later searchers after the Passage.

Like the search for a southern continent, the search for a northwest passage had been complicated by rumored sightings and discoveries that could not be found by later expeditions. Cook's successful charting of his first two voyages had awakened hopes of relocating some of these rumored discoveries and marking them with accuracy.

In planning another expedition to find the Northwest Passage, the Lords of the Admiralty were encouraged by two books, recently published in England, showing Russian discoveries in the north. The books included maps that purported to show the coastline of the far northwest coast of America, a part of the world previously as unknown as the islands of the South Pacific.

In 1728, a Dane named Vitus Bering commanded a Russian-sponsored expedition that sailed through the channel today known as the Bering Strait, which divides North America from Asia. Bering had not realized his discovery; fog kept him from seeing the coastline, and it was not certain whether he had found a bay or the final proof that Asia and America were separated by water. On a second voyage in 1741, Bering stopped at many of the islands in the Aleutian chain and sighted Mt. St. Elias on the North American coast. Bering died on the second trip, but his discoveries and maps were published in England in 1761 in a translation of a book written by Gerhard Friedrich Müller.

The second book that reached England around this time was written by Jacob von Stählin, who described the voyage of the Russian lieutenant Ivan Sindt, who reached the coast of North America in 1767. Von Stählin supplied what he called a "very accurate little map" that showed northwest America as many islands, the largest of which was called Alaschka.

The British Admiralty hoped that an expedition supplied with these maps could find its way through the islands to a waterway that flowed into Hudson Bay. To supplement this expedition, the Admiralty planned to send a second party across the Atlantic and into Hudson Bay. The hope was that the two parties could eventually link up with each other.

Clerke was slated to command the vessels that would cross the Pacific and sail around Alaschka. Yet though he was an experienced seaman, he had never been entrusted with such an important task. Really, England had only one man who had proved he could carry such a voyage through to a successful conclusion. But he had earned his retirement, and it would have seemed cruel to ask him to undertake a third major voyage.

So it was, according to Cook's early biographer, that a small dinner party came to be held. Present were Lord Sandwich, Sir Hugh Palliser, Philip Stephens, the Admiralty secretary, and Captain James Cook. The purpose of the party was to seek Cook's advice about the proposed attempt to find the Northwest Passage. The point was delicately raised as to the need for an experienced commander. As the story goes, Cook rose to announce his own willingness to command the new expedition. His offer was immediately accepted.

The Admiralty proceeded with haste. By July 1776 there was a firm plan for Cook to leave by the fall of that year. The hurriedly drawn plan allowed little time for delay—too little time, events would later prove.

Cook, accompanied by a second ship commanded by Clerke, would quickly make his way to the Cape of Good Hope, where he would take on provisions and leave by the end of October or beginning of November 1776. He would then search for the islands that du Fresne and Kerguelen reputedly had found in the South Indian Ocean.

Not spending "too much time in looking out for these

islands," he was to proceed to Tahiti, stopping at New Zealand if necessary, to give his crew additional refreshment. He was to leave Tahiti by February 1777, and go to "New Albion," the spot where Sir Francis Drake had reached the west coast of North America. He would then follow the coastline north to around 65°N. Arriving there in the month of June 1777, he was to explore "such rivers or inlets as may appear to be of a considerable extent and pointing towards Hudson's or Baffin's Bays." If Cook found such an inlet, he was to pass through it with the ships, if possible, or with some of the smaller vessels on board.

If Cook could find no such inlet in 1777, he was to winter in the Russian settlement at Kamchatka, or wherever else he might judge proper. The following spring, 1778, he was to make another try at discovering a passage that flowed from the Pacific to the Atlantic.

Cook was never a man who enjoyed leisure, but even he must have been pressed by the work that awaited him before departure. He was apparently unable to personally supervise the work being done on the two ships, the faithful *Resolution* and another cat-built ship, the *Discovery*, at the Royal Navy's shipyard at Deptford. The unfortunate result was that the ship-yard workers did a slovenly and incomplete job of preparing the two ships for the journey, something Cook would discover only after he had put to sea.

Perhaps at Cook's insistence, there would be few civilians on the new expedition. Omai, the Society Islander bound for home, would be one; the others would be John Webber, a painter, and William Bayly, the astronomer who had served on the *Adventure*. The scientific work would otherwise be taken care of by Cook and some of his officers.

One of these officers was James King, a brilliant and genial young man who had studied science at Paris and Oxford. King kept his own journal in which he reported meeting Cook and commenting to the captain that it was a shame no scientists would be on the third voyage. According to King, Cook replied, "Curse the scientists, and all science into the bargain!"

The comment indicates that Cook may already have been working too hard, but certainly also reflects the difficult time he had with Forster on the second voyage. Forster himself, when the story had been reported to him by King, wrote:

> I took the opportunity of setting things right by describing Cook's character and pointing out that it was in reality not so bad as it appeared, but that he was a cross-grained fellow who sometimes showed a mean disposition and was carried away by a hasty temper; and to this was added the overbearing attitude which was the result of having his head turned by Lord Sandwich.

King apparently disregarded Forster's "warning" and proved to be a loyal and valuable officer. Besides Second Lieutenant King, Cook's officers would include First Lieutenant John Gore, who had served on the *Endeavour*. The master of the ship was William Bligh, whose name would become synonymous with cruelty at sea. Cook's mixture of leniency and discipline on earlier voyages produced many good officers; on the third voyage Bligh would see a crueler side of Cook, and adopt that as a model.

The third lieutenant on the *Resolution* was a man named John Williamson. Though his name would not become a byword for cruelty like Bligh's, he was Bligh's equal in brutality. He often violated Cook's instructions concerning kind treatment of the islanders. His killing of a native on Hawaii was called by one of his shipmates "a cowardly, dastardly action for which Capt. Cook was very angry."

A sixteen-year-old midshipman, James Trevenen, wrote in

his journal: "Williamson is a wretch, feared and hated by his inferiors, detested by his equals, and despised by his superiors; a very devil, to whom none of our midshipmen have spoken for above a year." In the moment of the voyage's greatest crisis, when Cook faced a hostile mob on the beach at Hawaii, Williamson stood offshore in a boat; he directed his men to pull away. He never faced formal charges for his actions, but the lieutenant of marines later challenged him to a duel.

This lieutenant, Molesworth Phillips, commanded the twenty marines who shipped out on the *Resolution*. His sergeant and second-in-command was Samuel Gibson, one of the men who sailed on all three voyages with Cook. He had come a long way since the first voyage when, as a private, he had tried to desert at Tahiti. Trevenen wrote that Gibson was now "a great favorite" of Cook's.

II

BY THE END OF JUNE, Cook was ready to sail. There was an embarrassing problem: Clerke had signed a note for his brother's debts, and when the brother left England, Clerke was jailed. Such a proceeding was common in those days, and Clerke would eventually be released when settlement of the debt was made. The consequences, however, would prove fatal for Clerke: While in prison he contracted tuberculosis, and throughout the voyage would be debilitated by the disease.

Cook waited for a time in Plymouth Sound for Clerke to arrive. While he was at anchor there, he observed a fleet of sixty-two transport ships passing by; they carried a division of Hessian troops and horses on their way to quell the rebellion in the American colonies.

Cook finally left without the *Discovery* on July 12, leaving instructions that Clerke should follow with the *Discovery* and rejoin the *Resolution* at the Cape of Good Hope. Besides its complement of 112 men, the *Resolution* also had on board, at the request of King George, a bull, two cows, some calves, and a small herd of sheep. These were royal presents for Omai to take back to Tahiti. They would be a continual burden to Cook. His men were saddled with the additional work of caring for the animals, which were kept on deck most of the time. When the animals' appetites proved greater than expected, Cook had to stop at the Atlantic island of Tenerife to take on more fodder. It meant a five-day delay, and Cook was sailing on a tight schedule.

On August 14, the ship lost the northeast trade wind, and now spent sixteen days in the mid-Atlantic "doldrums," looking for the southeast trade wind that would take it to the Cape. Another exasperating delay, and by now the effects of the shoddy refitting at Deptford were appearing. The seams of the deck lost their caulking, leaving gaps so wide that rainwater fell through into the men's bunkrooms. The sailroom was also drenched, ruining some of the spare sails and requiring that the rest be spread on deck to dry.

Cook arrived at the Cape on October 18. Though he had ordered supplies months before, he found that nothing was ready. Bakers, who were supposed to have thousands of loaves ready for loading, had not carried out the order. They only began to fill it when they saw the *Resolution* in the bay.

Clerke arrived with the *Discovery* on November 10. His ship too showed major leaks, and the crews were set to work repairing the caulking that should have been done at Deptford.

Cook added livestock to the ship's floating zoo. They included two young bulls, two heifers, two horses, two mares, two rams, several ewes, goats, rabbits, and poultry. The *Resolu-*

tion and *Discovery* resembled Noah's arks, bound for the Pacific to populate the islands with animals, as Cook thought, that "might prove useful to posterity."

A month behind schedule, the two ships left the Cape on the thirtieth of November. Cook spent a month searching for the islands reported by Kerguelen and du Fresne. He found Kerguelen's Rendezvous Island on Christmas Day. Aside from a few other scattered islands, the month's sailing produced nothing of importance.

In the first two weeks of January 1777, Cook sailed through foggy weather—"in the dark"—was his way of describing it, for he was unable to check the chronometer against local time obtained from sightings of the sun and moon. Cook ordered the ships to run with full sail, probably because he was behind schedule (as King speculated in his journal), but it was a risk that led to an accident. A gust of wind ripped loose the fore topmast and the main topgallant mast of the *Resolution*. There was a day's delay for repairs.

On February 12, the two ships reached the familiar harbor of Queen Charlotte's Sound between the two main islands of New Zealand. The spot now had a sinister aspect for the crews, for the story of Furneaux's men killed and eaten by the Maoris there was on everyone's mind.

Cook proceeded as usual, setting up an observatory and tents for watering parties, supplying them with a guard.

Soon several canoes came alongside the ships. The islanders in them were unusually hesitant about approaching. One man whom Cook "had treated with remarkable kindness . . . when I was last here" would not respond to Cook's offer of presents. Cook realized that the Maoris knew that he was aware of the incident with Furneaux's men, and expected that Cook had at last come back for revenge.

Gradually Cook's open and kind treatment broke through the Maoris' reserve, and "a great many families came from different parts and took up their residence" near the men ashore. Among the visitors was a chief named Kahura; Furneaux had reported that he was the man who had led the attack on the seamen of the *Adventure*. The other Maoris by now had confirmed this, and urged Cook to kill him. "I believe," Cook wrote, "they were not a little surprised that I did not, for according to their ideas of equity this ought to have been done."

The Maoris were not the only ones who wanted to see Cook take vengeance. Some of his officers, including Gore, wrote in their journals that they thought the Maoris were contemptuous of the English because Cook allowed Kahura to live.

Most irate was Omai, who often urged Cook to shoot Kahura, and even offered to do it himself. After Kahura visited the ship with more than twenty members of his family, Omai indignantly asked Cook, "Why do you not kill him? You tell me if a man kills another in England he is hanged for it. This man has killed and yet you will not kill him, though a great many of his countrymen desire it and it would be very good."

Cook did question Kahura about the affair while the Maori chief was aboard the *Resolution*. "At this question," Cook wrote, "[Kahura] folded his arms, hung down his head, and looked like one caught in a trap. And I firmly believe [he] expected every moment to be his last, but was no sooner assured of his safety than he became cheerful."

After repeated questioning, Kahura told his side of the story. He said that one of Furneaux's men had taken a stone hatchet from him and offered nothing in return. Kahura then stole some bread to make up for the hatchet, and the boat's crew fired at him. Kahura was not hit, but another of the Maoris was killed. Kahura, realizing that it took time for the English to reload their guns, charged the commander of the boat. The other Maoris in the area followed, and the massacre took place.

Cook wrote in his journal that he did not believe Kahura's story, but he was determined to continue peaceful relations. He wrote:

> I had always declared to those who solicited his death that I had always been a friend to them all and would continue so unless they gave me cause to act otherwise; as to what was past, I should think no more of it as it was some time since and done when I was not there, but if ever they made a second attempt of that kind, they might rest assured of feeling the weight of my resentment.

Cook's stay was marked by the peace he hoped for, and on February 25, the ships sailed through the Cook Strait to the eastern side of New Zealand. Cook expected to find favorable trade winds that would take him quickly to Tahiti. But his previous experience with the winds was in June through August 1773. He now found that the prevailing trade winds in this season of the year blew in the opposite direction. He struggled against the wind, slowly coming to the conclusion that he could not possibly keep to the timetable set forth in his instructions.

At the end of March 1777, the ships put in at Atiu, one of the group of islands that are today named after Cook. Cook had sailed by them on his earlier voyages, and this was the first time he encountered the people there. The strain of the voyage may already have begun to tell, for Cook departed from his usual practice of leading the first group ashore.

Instead he sent Gore in charge of a party of three boats. Among the men were James Burney, now serving as first lieutenant of the *Discovery*, and William Anderson, surgeon of the *Resolution*. Anderson, as an educated European, believed in the existence of the noble savage, uncorrupted by civilization, and he wrote, "It was an opportunity I had long wished for, to see a people following the dictates of nature without being biased by education or corrupted by [meeting] more polished nations."

Turning the tables on Anderson, the islanders gently, but firmly, took the English into their custody and marched them around the island to meet its chiefs. At the hut of each chief, the English were entertained with dancing and ceremony.

Omai, undeceived by thoughts of noble savages, feared that he and his companions were going to be served up at a celebratory meal; at the sight of a fire, he asked if it had been made for that purpose. Anderson wrote that at Omai's question, the islanders "were greatly surprised and asked him if that was a custom with us."

Crowds of curious islanders gathered at each stop, asking the Englishmen to uncover their skin, "which commonly produced a universal murmur of admiration," Anderson wrote. "At the same time they did not miss these opportunities to rifle our pockets of everything and at last one of them snatched a small bayonet from Mr. Gore."

Burney and Anderson slipped away from the group and made their way back to the boats on the beach. There they found natives guarding the boats. The islanders took from Anderson some small pieces of coral and a few plants he had picked. Omai later explained that "it was not the custom here to admit freedoms of that kind [taking rocks and plants] till they had in some measure naturalized strangers to the country by entertaining them with festivity for two or three days."

Gore insisted that they could not stay for several days, and eventually they all returned to the ship with the report that the islanders had nothing they wanted to trade.

While at Atiu, Omai met with four men whom he recognized as people from the island of Raiatea, more than a thousand miles to the east. They had been in a canoe that had been swept out to sea some ten years before. Eventually, they drifted to Atiu. Cook heard of their journey with interest, because it

149

solved for him the problem of how so many people apparently of a common origin had come to populate the islands of the Pacific. Today's anthropologists agree with Cook's speculation.

Cook sailed on without further ado, for he was facing a serious problem. The cattle were near starvation, and he was still far to the west of Tahiti. Despite the urgings of his officers that he continue to fight the winds to proceed east, Cook made a crucial decision: He would give up the attempt to reach North America this year. There had been too many delays, and the important thing now was to replenish the ships' stores.

Even though Cook could not have known it, the expedition that was to try to find a passage through North America from the Atlantic was having its own difficulties. The ship *Lyon*, commanded by Richard Pickersgill (who had been with Cook on both his first and second voyages), had sailed from Deptford in May 1776. Pickersgill passed Greenland and found his way blocked by ice. He turned back and reached England at the end of October, less than six months after he departed. Pickersgill was court-martialed for drunkenness, and a second expedition was sent out to make the attempt to link up with Cook. It set out at about the same time Cook was on Atiu, but returned without success by the end of the summer.

Cook sailed west, in the direction the wind took him, and reached the Tonga Islands, where he had visited Eua and Tongatapu in 1773 and Nomuka in 1774.

The *Resolution* and *Discovery* arrived at Nomuka on April 28. Presently a man named Finau came aboard Cook's ship. He declared himself to be the king of all Tonga, enumerating some 153 islands in the group. Cook may have been skeptical, but it soon became clear that Finau was a man of considerable authority. He brought Cook and his officers to several of the nearby islands, at each of which they received gifts of pigs, turtles, and fowls. Cook likened Finau's manner to that of a man collecting tax.

The islanders entertained Cook's men with wrestling and boxing contests, including bouts between women. Some of Cook's men accepted challenges from islander men, but the Englishmen were always defeated. Burney wrote, "And as they did not take the drubbing with the moderation and good temper [that the losers in islander bouts showed], they were heartily laughed at."

At one of the islands Cook ordered a display of fireworks after darkness fell. Anderson estimated there were around five thousand natives present. After the fireworks, the islanders staged a display of dancing and singing. Tongans used drums and bamboo sticks for some of their dances. They struck the ground with different lengths of hollow bamboo to produce different tones.

Soon twenty women with crimson hibiscus flowers in their hair, and wearing dresses made of leaves dyed in many colors, performed a dance around the crew, in time to an ever-faster beat of the bamboo sticks.

Anderson viewed the dance primly: "As the quickness of the music increased they performed a sort of motion which with us would be rather reckoned indecent, as they moved the lower part of the body . . . from side to side for a considerable time with such vigor and dexterity as shows they have been well initiated in the practice of it."

Cook retained his usual objectivity toward island customs in describing the dance. He wrote, "These indecent actions, few as they are, do not arise from any wanton ideas, but merely to increase the variety, for it is astonishing to see the number of actions they observe in their dances and songs."

Learning of Cook's desire to trade for some red feather caps, Finau left on a trip to another island, promising to return with some. In his absence, the islanders became less friendly, and Cook decided to move on. On May 27, another important personage came alongside the *Resolution*.

This man identified himself as Fattafee, and he too claimed kingship over all the Tongas. Cook wrote, "As it was my interest . . . to pay my court to all these great men, without enquiring the legality of their titles," he promptly invited Fattafee on board.

The chief was aptly named, Cook wrote. He brought two fat hogs as a present to Cook, who wrote that the hogs were "not so fat as himself, for he was the most corpulent plump fellow we had met with." Yet Cook judged him a "sedate, sensible man" who asked good questions and paid close attention to the tour of the ship.

Omai resented Fattafee's claim to be king. Omai and Finau had exchanged names, a sign of mutual respect, and any diminution of Finau's power reflected badly on Omai. When Fattafee invited Cook ashore, Omai refused to go along. The matter was soon cleared up, for Finau again made his appearance. Cook invited both "kings" to dinner in his cabin, but "only Fattafee sat at table. Finau made his obeisance in the usual way and retired out of the cabin; this confirmed what [Fattafee] had before told us, that Finau could neither eat nor drink in his presence." Omai, Lieutenant King wrote, was "hurt at having taken a name that was not the highest."

Cook spent the summer among the Tonga Islands, making a chart of them and observing the customs of the islanders. When Fattafee and Finau were absent, however, stealing became a problem. Cook apparently was not so patient with it as he had earlier been, for some of the officers of both ships found his harshness disturbing. Thomas Edgar, the master of the *Discovery*, wrote of Cook's punishing islanders with up to six dozen lashes, and on one occasion of Cook's ordering a man's arms slashed below the shoulders with a knife, to mark him as a thief.

George Gilbert, an eighteen-year-old midshipman on the *Resolution*, whose father had been the ship's master on Cook's second voyage, wrote that "Captain Cook punished in a manner rather unbecoming of a European visit by cutting off their ears, firing at them with small shot or ball as they were swimming or paddling to the shore, and [ordering the crew] to beat them with the oars, and stick the boat hook into them wherever they could hit them."

On one occasion, when one of the goats and two turkeys were missing from the ship, Cook went so far as to seize Fattafee as a hostage. At first it appeared that some of the islanders would attack Cook, but Fattafee held them back with a wave of his hand. Before long the animals were returned. It was a tactic that Cook would try again, with less happy results.

Cook's conduct throughout his third voyage would appear to be inconsistent. At New Zealand he had refused to punish Kahura, who had killed Furneaux's men; here at Tonga he ordered severe punishments for relatively minor thefts. Compared to his two previous voyages, Cook's actions make it clear that he had too short a rest in England, that his age was beginning to tell, and that the balance between discipline and leniency that he formerly maintained was upset. He was not the same man.

Cook's journal reveals that he was less satisfied with the performance of his crew than on earlier voyages. In return, his officers seemed less admiring of their captain.

Williamson and Bligh, Cook's chief critics, went exploring on one of the islands and returned after two days, stripped of their muskets, ammunition, and other belongings. Before telling Cook of the loss, the two officers asked Omai to appeal to Fattafee and Finau for their return. Instead, now fearing

Cook's wrath, the chiefs fled the area. To persuade them to return, Cook sent a message that there would be no punishment for the theft. Previously, the theft of a musket was the one thing Cook was absolutely insistent on punishing.

Williamson was bitter at Cook's lenience, and complained to his journal that it was rumored that his gun had been stolen expressly for Finau. Williamson claimed that Cook had allowed Finau to keep the gun, "telling him that provided the natives did not steal from him, they should not be ill treated. . . . If a small nail was stolen from Capt. Cook, the thief if taken was most severely punished . . . [yet] with the loss of my gun . . . I could have no redress."

Cook's long stay at the islands gave him the opportunity to witness an unusual and solemn occasion: the installation of Fattafee's son as king, or what the islanders called "Tu'i Tonga." As part of the ceremony, Cook was told, both Fattafee and his son would eat a meal together, a unique moment, for no one was ever privileged to eat with the Tu'i Tonga except when the kingship changed hands.

The ceremony lasted two days. Cook and some of his officers were welcomed at the first part of it, which included processions, singing, and many rites involving food. After that part of the ceremony, Cook and his officers were shut up in a hut with a window through which they were told they could observe. This proved impossible, for the ceremony continued behind a fence that had been raised for the occasion.

Cook was unusually determined to find out the details of the event. He stayed on the island overnight, and slipped out of the hut several times, only to encounter guards who barred his way, telling him, "*tabu, tabu,*" a word that he well knew had religious significance.

At one point, Cook was asked to depart with all his men to the ships, for soon every place on the island would be *tabu*.

Cook argued the point, and on learning that he would be allowed to observe if he removed his clothing above the waist and let his hair hang loose, he immediately complied. Williamson described the scene that followed:

> We who were on the outside were not a little surprised at seeing Capt. Cook in the procession of the chiefs, with his hair hanging loose and his body naked down to the waist. . . . I do not pretend to dispute the propriety of Capt. Cook's conduct, but I cannot help thinking he rather let himself down.

Cook had been in the Pacific as long as any European had ever been; it was by now a second home to him, and he had discovered more of its secrets than any living person. No islander had been to all the places he had seen; few if any Europeans looked upon the peoples of the Pacific with such an open and understanding heart. Perhaps it was the ceremony of the Tu'i Tonga that completed the sense of separation that Cook may have felt. In his journal Cook began to use "we" to refer to himself and the other chiefs and nobles inside the compound. He wrote of the ceremony that took place:

> On some signal being given we all started up and ran several paces to the left and sat down with our backs to the prince and the few who remained with him and I was [asked] not to look behind me. Neither this commandment nor the remembrance of Lot's wife discouraged me from facing about when I saw the prince had turned his face to the *marae*. But this last movement had brought so many people between him and me that I could not see well what he was doing; but was afterward told that the king and prince were each presented with a piece of

roasted yam. This was the more probable as all the people turned their backs to them at this time [so they would not see them eating].

The ceremony soon concluded with wrestling and boxing matches, and Cook was allowed to examine the utensils that had been part of the ceremony. These had previously been *tabu*, "but the ceremony being over they became simply what they really were, viz. empty baskets." Cook asked many other questions about the ceremony, but seldom got any other answers than *tabu*.

The wind now blew strongly toward the east, and Cook took advantage of it to make the passage to Tahiti. On the journey, however, both ships were severely damaged by a storm. The *Discovery's* mainmast was sprung, and would require a safe harbor for replacement.

III

THE SHIPS WERE IN SIGHT of Tahiti by August 12. Cook put in at Vaitepiha Bay, intending to get fresh food there before proceeding to his familiar base at Matavai Bay.

Cook had grown fond of Omai on the voyage from England, and hoped to resettle him on his home island in a way that would ensure his happiness and security. The first meeting with the Tahitians showed Cook how difficult that would be. Among the first islanders to come aboard were a chief called Utai and a man who was a relative of Omai's. Neither paid much attention to Omai at first, but when Omai showed them his stock of red feathers they became his closest friends. Cook wrote, "It was evident to everyone [except Omai] that it was not the man but his property they were in love with." Omai soon acquired a train of followers who, Cook could see, would stay with Omai only as long as his stock of feathers held out.

There was news of greater concern to Cook: Two other great sailing ships had twice visited Vaitepiha Bay since Cook had last been there. Proof was a house that the visitors had erected; nearby was the grave of one of the ships' commanders.

The islanders said the ships had come from a country called Rema. Cook correctly deduced that they had sailed from Lima, Peru, and that they were Spanish. The first ship had left two priests and a soldier to begin the conversion of the islanders to Catholicism. The commander had taken four islanders to Peru for instruction in the Catholic faith; two of these survived the return voyage.

The house had since been deserted, but Cook found a cross standing in front of it inscribed with Latin words that translated: "Christ conquers; Charles III rules, 1774." Cook ordered another Latin inscription carved on the back of the cross. It translated simply: "George III, King; years 1767, 69, 73, 74 & 77," establishing England's prior claims. Cook realized that he was now competing with both the French and the Spanish for rights in the Pacific.

The Spanish had taken the missionaries back to Peru, and Cook found no trace of the two islanders who had been instructed as Catholics. The Spanish had told the Tahitians not to let the English ships enter Vaitepiha Bay, but "they were so far from paying any regard to it that [the local chief] now made me a formal surrender of the province and everything in it." To seal the agreement, Cook and the young chief embraced and exchanged names.

On August 23, Cook's ships sailed for Matavai Bay; the *Resolution* reached it the same evening, but the crippled *Discovery* did not arrive till the next morning. Cook's old friend Otoo, accompanied by a great many canoes full of his people, came to greet the English.

Otoo was preparing for war with Maheine, the chief of the neighboring island of Moorea. Before long an islander from another district brought the news that Spanish ships had just now come to anchor in Vaitepiha Bay. Cook sent a boat to reconnoiter, but the rumor proved to be false. Cook determined that Maheine's men had spread the rumor to drive Cook away.

Towha, the chief whom Cook saw commanding the war fleet on the previous voyage, now came to tell Otoo that a human sacrifice to their god Eatua was in readiness as part of the preparations for the war. Otoo quickly left with Towha, followed by Cook, Anderson, Webber the artist, and Omai.

The ceremony, held on a tiny island offshore, lasted for two days. Cook was relieved of the moral dilemma of deciding whether he should interfere, for by the time he arrived the man to be sacrificed was already dead. Cook stayed for the entire two days, recording the details of what he saw.

Sacred objects, including a casket containing an effigy of Eatua, were carried out by island priests. The eye of the sacrificed man was removed from his body and offered to Otoo. The chief made eating motions, but Cook noticed that he did not actually eat it. A kingfisher, a sacred bird, cried out in the trees, and Otoo said with great satisfaction, "There is the Eatua." When the victim's body was buried, a boy made a squeaking noise, which was again interpreted as the voice of Eatua.

On the second day of the ceremony, Cook recognized that the visits of Europeans had already had a corrupting influence on the Tahitian religion. Among the sacred objects that were brought forth were some ostrich feathers that Cook had presented to Otoo on the second voyage. Then the *maro*, or royal belt, was taken out. Cook noted that it consisted of many kinds of feathers attached to a base which was obviously the remnant of a British flag. He had reason to believe it was the flag Wallis had planted ashore signifying English possession of the island.

Cook had not previously believed that the Tahitians practiced human sacrifice, but he now found that the forty-nine skulls at this particular *marae* came from similar victims. The discovery also explained the presence of skulls at the other *maraes* Cook had seen in the Society Islands.

Towha asked Cook if he thought the sacrifice had been a good one, and if the English practiced such customs. Cook "told the chief that this sacrifice was so far from pleasing the *Eatua* as they intended that he would be angry with them for it, and that they would not succeed against Maheine." Omai added that if "a chief in England had put a man to death . . . that he would be hanged for it." To all this Towha shouted "*maeno, maeno,*" ["vile, vile"] and refused to listen to another word. Cook wrote that "we left him with as great a contempt of our customs as we could possibly have of theirs."

Cook's prediction of the outcome of the war was not a rash one. He observed that the Tahitians seemed divided over the wisdom of the war, and Cook concluded that success under these conditions was unlikely. His judgment proved correct some days later when Towha led his ships against Maheine's. In the midst of battle, Towha sent word to Otoo that he needed reinforcements, but the chief did not send help and Towha was forced to withdraw. Cook heard rumors that Towha was planning to overthrow Otoo when the English departed. Cook let it be known that if any harm came to Otoo, the ships would return and punish the rebels.

Cook had wanted to witness the battle in person, but a painful attack of rheumatism kept him confined to the ship. Some time later Otoo's mother, three of his sisters, and eight other women came aboard and announced that they could cure the captain.

Out of curiosity Cook "submitted myself to their direction." They had him lie down in his cabin, and then "as many as could get round me began to squeeze me with both hands from head to foot . . . till they made my bones crack and a perfect mummy of my flesh—in short after being under their hands about a quarter of an hour I was glad to get away from them." Soon afterward, however, Cook's pain did lessen, and he underwent the treatment several more times, after which he found the rheumatism had entirely disappeared.

Once again the time came for Cook to bid farewell to his friend Otoo. Otoo told Cook that the Spanish had talked of making a permanent settlement on the island, but assured Cook, "They shall not come to Matavai, for it belongs to you." Otoo's attitude indicated how little aware the islanders were of the effect that contact with Europeans would have.

"This shows," Cook wrote, "with what facility a settlement . . . might be made among them, which for the regard I have for them I hope will never happen." Cook's hopes were in vain. In 1797, the London Missionary Society would establish the first permanent European settlement at Matavai Bay. With the Europeans came prostitution, drunkenness, diseases, and involvement in the political quarrels of Europe. By 1880 Tahiti was a French colony.

Cook's ships made the one-day journey to the island of Moorea, where Otoo's enemy Maheine ruled. Cook was surprised to find a fine harbor there. Streams flowing into the bay gave ready access to fresh water, and the banks were covered with hibiscus trees, which were useful for firewood. The bay was dominated by the volcanic highlands of the interior, making it a beautiful and romantic spot. Otoo and his people had always told Cook that there was no suitable anchorage for his ships at Moorea; he realized now that the advice had been intended to keep him from forming an alliance with Maheine.

While the ships stood at anchor, Maheine himself came to pay a visit. He approached with some caution, but Cook welcomed both him and his wife aboard and gave them gifts appropriate for a royal couple. They sent to shore for a pig to present to Cook, and the exchange of gifts continued.

Nonetheless, a day or two later one of the goats aboard ship was stolen. Cook sent a messenger to find the chief, only to discover that he and most of the islanders were now *mata-ou*. Cook considered simply departing, but decided that would give "encouragement to the people of the other islands . . . to rob us with impunity."

The actions that Cook now took seem out of proportion to the loss of a single goat. He went inland with a group of 35 armed men, ordering three other boats of men to circle the island and meet him on the other side. As Cook progressed through the interior, he burned houses and canoes wherever he found them. Some of the destroyed canoes were large boats, capable of carrying 100 to 120 men. Even so, Cook did not find the goat.

Returning to the ship, Cook sent a native messenger to find Maheine and tell him that the English would continue to destroy the islanders' possessions until the goat was returned. Finally, it was, and although Cook wrote that he "regretted" the incident, it caused disquiet among his own men. George Gilbert, who had heard stories of a different Cook from his father, wrote that Cook "seemed to be very rigid in the performance of his order which everyone executed with the greatest reluctance except Omai. . . . I can't well account for Capt. Cook's proceedings on this occasion as they were so very different from his conduct in like cases in his former voyages."

Cook was satisfied with the effect his actions had on the islanders. When the ships anchored at Owharre Harbor at Omai's home island of Huaheine, Cook heard Omai retell the story of the destruction at Moorea, exaggerating greatly the number of houses and canoes that had been destroyed. "I saw it had great effect upon all who heard it," Cook wrote, "so that I had hopes they would behave a little better than they usually had done at this island."

Cook now gave Omai shrewd advice: to share his possessions with two or three of the principal chiefs to secure their protection. Cook remarked, "It is here as in many other countries. A man that is richer than his neighbor is sure to be envied. This was Omai's fate, and there were numbers who wished to see him upon a level with themselves. From these he had everything to fear."

Cook saw to it that Omai made presents to the local chief, a boy about ten years old. In return the chief gave Omai a good-sized plot of land, where the *Resolution*'s people set to work building him a house and planting a garden.

An unfortunate incident made a new enemy for Omai. A man stole a sextant from one of the observatory tents. When Omai pointed out the thief, Cook took the man aboard the *Resolution*, where his conduct was that of a "hardened scoundrel" and so "I punished him with greater severity than I had ever done anyone before." He ordered the man's ears cut off.

Released, the man went ashore and destoyed Omai's garden, and then announced that when Cook left he would kill Omai and burn his house. Cook had to take the man aboard again and imprison him, intending to put him off at an island to the north.

The ship's crew now helped Omai carry off the presents his noble friends had given him in England. Cook regarded them with a wry eye:

Among many other useless things was a box of toys . . . which seemed to please the gazing multitude very much; but as to his pots, kettles, dishes, plates, drinking mugs, glasses, etc., etc., etc. hardly anyone so much as looked at. Omai himself now found that they were of no manner of use to him—that a baked hog eat better than a boiled one, that a plantain leaf made as good a dish . . . as pewter, and that a coconut shell was as good to drink out of.

Omai pleaded with Cook for firearms, pointing out that he would need them to defend himself. Against his better judgment Cook left him pistols, muskets, ammunition, and powder.

The enemy of Omai, held in chains aboard the *Resolution*, escaped. Cook discovered that the men on watch had fallen asleep and the man took the key to free himself "which made it necessary to punish those that were at fault."

The punishments were the most severe Cook ever inflicted on his own men. William Harvey, the master's mate who had sailed with Cook on all three voyages, was demoted to midshipman and sent on board the *Discovery*. The sentinel and quartermaster "have been kept in irons and flogged every day since," according to Bayly two days later.

Cook's final farewell to Omai was a moving occasion. Lieutenant King told Cook that Omai wept all the time the boat was taking him ashore. Cook noted in his journal that Omai's faults were "more than overbalanced by his great good nature and docile disposition. . . . grateful heart . . . tolerable share of understanding [without] application and perseverance to exert it."

Cook regretted that Omai had not learned more useful skills during his stay in England. He also felt that the people of Tonga had many accomplishments that Omai might have learned and brought home to his own people. But he did not expect that Europe could change the islanders' ways to any great extent.

The principal benefits that the islands would receive from Omai's travels, thought Cook, "will be in the animals that have been left upon them. . . . When these multiply of which I think there is little doubt, they will equal if not exceed any place in the known world for provisions." Yet there was evidence all around him that the islanders had one thing in plenty, and that was food.

When the master of the *Resolution*, William Bligh, returned in command of the ship *Bounty* eleven years later, he learned that Omai had distinguished himself in battle with the islands of Raiatea and Bora Bora, and secured a victory for Huaheine with his firearms.

Contrary to Cook's expectations, the islanders said to Bligh that they "received a great deal of information from Omai. They . . . say he knew and showed them a great many things." Three years after Cook's departure Omai died of a disease. After his death, his house and garden were destroyed. And as for Cook's attempts to stock the islands with European animals, a missionary in 1829 reported, "The animals, with the exception of the dogs and pigs, have all died."

Cook sailed on to the island of Raiatea, making harbor there on November 4, to the usual friendly reception. Petty thieving soon began, and Cook's men now showed signs of being completely out of control.

Williamson, according to Bayly, caught an islander who had stolen a nail, and ordered him stretched out on the deck. Williamson "attempted to jump on his head, but the man avoided him, but [Williamson] stamped his foot on the side of the Indian's face in the most unhuman manner and broke several of his teeth out."

A marine deserted the ship, and the islanders fled. Cook personally went ashore to recover the man, and ordered him to be punished with a dozen lashes for two consecutive days.

The example did not stop the desertions. On the twenty-fourth two men from the *Discovery* slipped ashore. One of them was Alexander Mouat, a fifteen-year-old midshipman, the son of Captain Patrick Mouat, who had commanded one of the ships on Byron's circumnavigation. The old man was still alive in England, and the news of his son's desertion would be a shock and a disgrace.

Alexander Home, the master's mate on the *Discovery*, reported that Cook now assembled the companies of both ships together and made a long speech, which Home describes:

> He made use both of entreaties and threats and with a deal of art and eloquence, for he could speak much to the purpose. . . . Among other things he told them they might run off if they pleased. But they might depend upon it he would recover them again, that in such a case he had [only] to seize the chiefs and although [the islanders] might like them very well to stay . . . he knew for certain that they liked their chiefs far better. . . . They all must know that his authority over these isles was so great that never [did a man have] a people more under his command or at his devotion. . . . His authority would bring them back, and dead or alive he'd have them.

Though Cook did seize the relatives of the king of Raiatea, thereby bringing the deserters back to the ship, he was making an important miscalculation about the limits of his own power. Indeed, the Raiateans made an attempt to turn the tables and kidnap both Cook and Clerke at the watering place where

Cook went to take a bath every evening; the Raiateans failed, but in Hawaii Cook's tactic of taking hostages in response to a theft would lead to disaster.

Cook was by now anxious to make his way to North America, getting an early start on the season. The preceding year had been a failure, in terms of what Cook had set out to do, and he did not intend to fail again. He instructed Clerke that in case the ships became separated, Clerke was to search no more than five days for the *Resolution* before proceeding on the search for the passage through North America.

Again, though, the winds blew opposite the direction Cook wanted to go, and by the time the ships crossed the equator they were farther to the west than when they had left the Society Islands. On December 24 the ships sighted a new island that Cook named Christmas Island, part of the thousand-mile-long group today called the Line Islands.

It was a barren spot, inhabited only by giant sea turtles. The ships stopped there to gather turtle meat. Seventeen-year-old midshipman Trevenen described the sea-turtle hunts in his journal. The small boats that ventured forth were surrounded by voracious sharks. One of them took the rudder of Trevenen's boat in its teeth and Trevenen battled it with his "hanger" (sword) to free the boat.

Nearer the shore the sharks were not a problem, and Cook's men dove into the water to catch the turtles in the pools of water in which they hid. "Often," Trevenen wrote, "one [man] was not strong enough to hold them. He would be dragged along, sometimes up, sometimes down, till others came to his assistance." Cook's men took more than three hundred turtles, weighing ninety to one hundred pounds apiece.

On the eighteenth of January, 1778, two more islands appeared on the horizon. They were part of the Hawaiian Islands, which Cook first named after his patron Lord Sandwich. Cook soon found himself greeted by canoes, and was "agreeably surprised" to find that the occupants spoke a language similar to that of the Society Islanders. They were in fact part of the Polynesian people, whose ancestors had populated the islands of the eastern Pacific some thousand years earlier.

Cook invited some of the islanders aboard and deduced from "the wildness of their looks and actions" that they had never been on board a ship before. The islands were far from the track that Spanish and Portuguese traders used to cross the Pacific, and Cook was the first European to land there.

Searching for a harbor, Cook sent Williamson to the shore with a party of men. The curious islanders swarmed about the boat. Williamson thought they were attempting to steal muskets and oars. Bayly, one of the party, thought they were merely eager to help. Williamson ordered the men to drive off the islanders with musket fire, and one of the Hawaiians was killed.

The *Resolution* was too far away for Cook to observe what happened. Williamson, citing his "differences of conscience" with Cook over proper treatment of the islanders, did not tell Cook of the incident until after the ships left Hawaii.

Soon afterward the two ships came to Waimea Bay, off the island of Kauai. Cook went ashore with a party of three boats. As usual the captain was unarmed, but as he stepped ashore something strange, even to his experience, happened: All the islanders "fell flat on their faces, and remained in that humble posture till I made signs to them to rise."

Setting his men to the task of bringing empty casks to a fresh-water pond inland, Cook began to explore the island. Wherever he went a Hawaiian ran ahead to announce his arrival, "and everyone whom we met fell on their faces and remained in this position till we had passed."

Cook came to a place similar to the Tahitians' *maraes*, though the Hawaiians called them *heiaus*, and found evidence of human sacrifices. Nearby was a large house that held an altar flanked by carved figures of women. Cook understood from the islanders that these were goddesses, but he doubted that the islanders worshipped the images themselves "as they had no objections to our . . . examining them." He was yet to comprehend that the islanders regarded him as a god himself.

Cook met similar treatment at the neighboring island of Niihau. He was eager to learn more about these new people and to chart the island group, but these activities were time-consuming, and he decided to make for his main goal—the continent of North America. But he would return.

I V

ON FEBRUARY 2 THE SHIPS left Hawaii and by March 7, the "long-looked-for coast of New Albion was seen." New Albion was Sir Francis Drake's name for the place where he had reached North America, thought today to be south of Cook's landfall.

Soon after Cook's arrival, squalls and storms struck the ships; Cook named the nearest point of land Cape Foul Weather. This was on the coast of what is now the state of Oregon. Three thousand miles to the east, George Washington's troops were fighting British redcoats to create the nation that would eventually stretch westward to this spot.

Cook clung as close to the shoreline as he could, fighting winds and stormy weather, looking for a harbor. He soon sighted a point of land that he named Cape Perpetua after the saint whose feast day is March 7. It still bears that name, near Highway 101 north of the town of Roosevelt Beach.

On March 22 the ships sighted what appeared to be a bay.

Cook wrote that it "flattered us with hopes of finding a harbor. These hopes lessened as we drew nearer. . . . On this account I called the point of land to the north of it Cape Flattery." The northwest tip of the state of Washington is still marked by the name Cook gave it.

Night fell as the ships sailed past Cape Flattery and in the darkness they sailed past the strait that separates Washington State from Vancouver Island—named for George Vancouver, then a midshipman on the *Discovery*, who in the years 1790 to 1795 would survey this coast in his own ship. In missing the strait Cook missed one of the rumored waterways that Müller's book claimed led to a large inland sea, and the Northwest Passage. Cook wrote, "We saw nothing like it, nor is there the least probability that ever any such thing existed." It did not exist as a passage through North America, but it is a large channel for Cook to have missed, even at night in a storm.

On March 29 Cook saw the tip of a peninsula he called Woody Point, but which bears the name Cape Cook today. Nearby there was a bay; Cook drew nearer and saw the first sign of inhabitants, approaching in canoes "without showing the least mark of fear or distrust." These were the people who called their part of the coast Nootka.

Edward Riou, a seventeen-year-old midshipman on the *Discovery*, thought the Nootka people

a set of the dirtiest beings ever beheld, their faces and hair being a lump of red and black earth and grease, their bodies covered with the skins of animals. . . . In the canoe that first came alongside was a man that stood up and held forth a long while. . . . His oratory did not seem to be the best in the world. . . . On his head he wore a kind of hat made of cane and in shape resembling a buck's head . . . he presented it for sale as well as several other things, which at once convinced us they were no novices at that business. In return for his hat he had a large axe and left . . . quite content.

It was true that these people were acquainted with European visitors; the Spanish captain Juan Perez had been here in 1774. Being experienced traders, according to Cook, they were not "fond of" beads and rejected cloth. They wanted iron more than anything else, and Cook noted that they used it to forge their own tools and weapons.

In the morning other people came bearing more valuable trading goods—a wide variety of furs, including many that the Nootkas had acquired from other tribes inland. Cook and his men saw only raccoons and minks ashore, but the Nootkas brought furs of sea otter, bear, fox, wolf, wildcat (cougar), deer, marten, ermine, squirrel, and seal. The rich variety of furs offered to Cook would spark the beginning of the English fur trade on this coast. Seven years later Nathaniel Portlock, the master's mate of the *Discovery*, would command a ship sent to open the fur trade along the northwest coast.

The Nootkas offered other, less desirable, objects. According to Bayly, these included "three or four human hands which . . . appeared to have been lately cut off as the flesh was . . . raw. They made signs that they were good eating."

Each day's trading began with a ceremony much like that described by Riou. As the first canoes approached, a leader would stand up with a spear or rattle in his hand. Sometimes he had his face covered with a totem or mask. He would deliver a speech punctuated by his rowers' cries, called "hallooing" by the English. Burney described the effect:

They paddle in most excellent time. The foremost man every 3rd or 4th stroke [makes] flourishes with his paddle. The halloo is a single note in which they all join, swelling it out in the middle and letting the sound die away. In a calm with the hills around us, it had an effect infinitely superior to what might be imagined from anything so simple.

The Nootkas were not beyond deception. When they found that Cook's crews desired animal oil, they began to bring bladder skins filled with it; some of the skins were later found to contain water.

On other occasions the Nootkas brought skillfully made models of animals and birds that they apparently used as decoys for hunting. One of the Nootkas increased the value of a model of a bird's head by shaking it up and down while another man secretly blew a small whistle, making it seem as if the bird were doing the whistling. The English seaman who gave "ten times the value" for it soon discovered that he had been tricked.

Cook was less concerned with the Nootkas' dishonesty than with the corruption of the English navy's shipyards. He received a report that nearly all the masts of both ships were rotten because poor quality wood was used in the refitting. Fortunately there were many tall trees ashore that could be used as replacements, but the necessary work cost the voyage time.

Cook used the time to explore, again carefully noting the customs of the people. Once he saw the entry of other people into the bay in a canoe. A group of Nootkas approached the visitors and drew up their canoe as if for battle. Instead, each group began singing in turn, and after a time the two groups parted and the strangers left the area. "Our first friends," Cook wrote, "seemed determined to [keep] us entirely to themselves."

Cook was informed that the Nootkas were demanding payment for the water and wood collected by his men. He went to the place where grass was being cut to provide fodder for the goats and sheep still aboard ship, and asked for the owner of the grass. A dozen men stepped forward. Cook paid them, but another group arrived and claimed ownership. Cook paid these men as well, but each payment brought new "pretended proprietors . . . and there was not a blade of grass that had not a separate owner, so that I very soon emptied my pockets with purchasing, and when they found I had nothing more to give they let us cut wherever we pleased."

The refitting of the masts completed, Cook made ready to sail again. On April 26, despite a falling barometer that indicated the approach of a storm, he decided to leave. The storm, which struck soon afterward, was worse than Cook expected. It blew the ships well off the coast, and to make matters worse, the *Resolution* sprung a leak that flooded the rooms where bread and fish were stored. Quick work with the pumps soon brought the leak under control.

It was a week before the ships regained sight of the rocky, mountainous coast. In many places, snow covered the land down to the sea, and Cook kept well away. He recognized Mt. St. Elias, discovered by Bering, from the location and description laid down by the Danish explorer. It seemed to give credence to the maps in Müller's book, purportedly those made by Bering.

Soon, however, Cook found that the coastline seemed to turn sharply to the southwest. He began to search for an inlet that would take him north. He anchored at a place he called Hinchingbrook Island, where two canoes approached the ship. Cook was fascinated by the construction of the craft: "The frame only was of wood . . . and the outside seal skin." Cook called the people Eskimos, the name Bering had given them; their boats were a type known as the *umiak*.

The boatsmen were clothed in sealskin dresses reaching nearly to the knee. As they approached the ship they displayed a white dress and opened their arms in a friendly gesture. Cook and his officers imitated the gesture, and threw presents into the boats. One of the presents was a glass bowl, with which the Eskimos were so delighted they gave Cook "one of their frocks which was . . . exceedingly well calculated to keep out both wet and cold; then both boats put off and made for the shore, [the Eskimos] paddling and singing with all the jollity imaginable. We either found these good folk on one of their jubilee days, or they are a very happy race."

As Cook found himself compelled by the coastline to sail farther south, his frustration grew. The *Resolution*'s leak now grew worse, and Cook was obliged to turn into a large inlet that he called Sandwich Sound—today's Prince William Sound. Finding an anchorage, Cook had the *Resolution* heeled over (pulled over at an angle) to expose the port side of the hull, where the leak seemed to be. The carpenters removed the metal sheathing to find that the seams between the planks of the hull had not been caulked at all by the shipyard workers at Deptford. In some places the gaps between planks were 2½ inches wide.

While the carpenters repaired the hull, Cook set up a trade with the Eskimos. He was especially eager to obtain more of their skin "dresses," because his men found them lighter and stronger than, and equally waterproof as, their own British-made oilskins.

The Eskimos wore mittens made of the skin of bear paws; many of them wore high cone-shaped hats made of wicker and ornamented with sky blue glass beads about the size of large peas. Other head coverings were carved from wood in the shape of a seal's head. The women had their chins and cheeks tattooed or stained in a way designed to mimic beards.

Most unusual was the custom of both men and women of cutting slits through their lower lips large enough to stick their tongues through. When one of the seamen saw a native sticking his tongue through this slit, he called out that here was a man with two mouths, "and indeed," Cook wrote, "it does not look unlike it." Some of the people inserted pieces of bone through this slit, from which they suspended a cord on which decorative pieces of bone or beads were attached. "This ornament is a very great impediment to the speech," wrote Cook, "and makes them look as if they had a double row of teeth in the under jaw."

The Eskimos also pierced the cartilage of their noses with bones or cords, and their ears were pierced not just in the lobes but all around, with more pieces of bone from which they hung beads and small bones. They also wore bracelets and other ornaments "and to crown all they use both black and red paint," Cook wrote, "so that I have nowhere seen Indians that take more pains to ornament, or rather disfigure themselves, than these people."

An examination of some of the natives' sky blue beads showed Cook that they were made of glass, indicating that they came from a nation that had manufacturing facilities. Cook decided that the beads must have been obtained from some place north of here, where the Russians had trading posts.

By the seventeenth of May the ship was fit for sailing again, and Cook spent more than a month in the futile search for an inlet that would take him north. He turned back each time, finding that as the ships proceeded north through the inlets, the water changed from salt to fresh—a sign that there was no passage through to the sea.

On June 25 the ships reached the end of the Alaskan Peninsula and came to the beginning of the Aleutian Island chain. This position was by no means clear to Cook, who realized that the Russian maps were grossly inaccurate, and he was wary of sailing up yet another blind inlet in search of a channel. He sailed past several islands, trying to determine the geography.

On the morning of the twenty-sixth, the weather was thick

with a fog so dense that the men could not see more than a hundred yards ahead. Cook took another of the chances that would have daunted a lesser commander, and once again his amazing luck held. "As the wind was now very moderate," he wrote, "I decided to run." That is, he set the ships on a northward course to pass through what promised to be a channel to open sea.

The fog deepened, and when the crew heard the sound of waves breaking on rocks, the ships lay anchor and stood till the fog lifted. In a few hours, when the weather cleared, "it was perceived we had escaped very imminent danger," Cook wrote with customary understatement. Midshipman Gilbert was more candid: "We could not help being struck with horror at the sight of the dangers we had escaped."

Behind the ships lay a narrow channel which contained two high rocks about a mile apart. Miraculously the two ships had threaded the channel in a fog so dense that the masters of the ships could not agree whether they had passed between the rocks, or to one side of them. Cook admitted that he would never have attempted to pass through the channel even on a clear day.

The ships were still not free of danger. They seemed to be surrounded by land in every direction. To the southwest lay a ridge of mountains that extended beyond sight, on an island that Cook named Providence, to commemorate his escape from the rocks. When he found out the Eskimo name for it, he crossed out Providence and wrote Oonalaschka on his chart. This was Unalaska Island, one of the largest in the Aleutians.

A violent tide now combined with unfavorable winds to press the ships back. Cook anchored at a harbor called Samgoonoodha by the Eskimos. He would return there on the trip back from the polar ice cap.

By July 2 Cook realized that he had broken through to open

sea. It was in fact the Bering Sea, and a look at a modern map shows that Cook could have sailed northeast across the broad expanse of water he was later to call Bristol Bay. That would have saved him a great deal of time, but he had no maps that he could rely on, and feared that sailing north would bring him to the coast of Asia. Laboriously the two ships kept to the coast, sailing back up the northern side of the Alaskan Peninsula. It was the only way Cook had of making sure he was still off North America.

The journey was not a wasted one. Though Bering and others had been here before Cook, he would be the first to make an accurate outline of the coast of Alaska that others (including three future captains among the ships' companies) would be able to follow with the assurance that they were true.

Cook could travel faster now because he no longer had to explore each inlet to find a way north. By July 9 the ships had reached the end of the peninsula, at a river Cook called Bristol. "It must abound with salmon," the captain wrote, "as we saw many leaping in the sea before it and some were found in the maw of cod we had caught." The river is now known as Kvichak, and the bay in which the ships stood known as Kvichak Bay. Today salmon canneries dot its shores.

Müller's maps showed that the ships were now sailing over a large expanse of land; Stählin's maps showed a great many islands here. Cook found only one island, and looked in vain for more.

A blow to the men's spirits came with the death of the *Resolution*'s surgeon, William Anderson. He had known for over a year that he had been suffering from incurable tuberculosis, but tried to keep the secret from the others until his weakened condition made it obvious. He had been a friend to all aboard ship, and his learning in botany and the Tahitian language made him a valuable man to Cook. Though the hardships of the journey hardened the voyagers to death, they remained sensitive to the loss of a friend and a gentle man.

The day Anderson's body was committed to the sea was a gloomy one, foggy with a cold drizzling rain, expressing the feelings of the crews. The shore had only a greenish hue to remind them that it was the height of summer in England.

On August 9 the ships reached the end of Seward Peninsula, the point at which Asia and North America almost touch. Cook called the place Cape Prince of Wales, noting that it was "the western extremity of all America hitherto known."

The ships crossed the narrow Bering Strait and found an anchorage on the Chukchi Peninsula in Asia, at what is now known as Lavrentiya Bay. Near the north shore of the bay stood a village. Cook could see its inhabitants fleeing with burdens on their backs. He set out with three boats of armed men toward the village, but as he approached the shore he faced a rear guard of forty to fifty men armed with harpoons and bows. When the boats landed, the men ashore lost their confidence and retreated.

"I followed them alone," Cook wrote, "without anything in my hand, and by signs and actions got them to stop and receive some trifles I presented them with, and in return they gave me two fox skins and a couple of [walrus tusks]."

Cook departed and sailed north, keeping both coasts in sight for the next two days. He suspected, but could not yet conclude, that he was in sight of two continents—the village he had visited might be on an island, and the people of Chukchi were similar in many ways to their neighbors in North America.

On the afternoon of August 13, a breeze sprang up that carried the ships northward out of sight of land for a few hours, until they steered northeast and back along the northern shoreline of North America. Cook now knew he had achieved his goal of rounding the northern coast.

The ships crossed the Arctic Circle, and by the seventeenth the men could see both the sun and moon in the sky at noon. At about the same time, wrote Cook, "we perceived a brightness in the northern horizon like that reflected from ice, commonly called the blink."

If the sighting did prove to be the northern ice pack, it would mean that the ice around the North Pole began at a point much farther away from the pole than the ice pack surrounding the South Pole. It would be a crushing blow to hopes for finding a northwest passage, for it would mean that the sea route across the top of North America was blocked by ice even in the summer.

Lieutenant King had expressed the optimism felt a few days earlier, when it became clear they had rounded the northwest tip of North America: "We already begin to compute the distance of our situation from known parts of Baffin's Bay." Baffin Bay was the intended destination of the ship that was supposed to cross the Atlantic to meet them. Now, two hours after the first sight of the "blink," the ships saw the ice fields dead ahead, at a latitude of 70°41′N. "The ice was quite impenetrable," Cook wrote, "and extended from west by south to east by north as far as the eye could reach."

A favorable wind took the ships eastward along the edge of the ice pack as Cook searched for a passage through.

On August 18 Cook reached the farthest north he would ever attain: 70°44′N. "We were at this time in 20 fathoms water, close to the edge of the ice which was as compact as a wall and seemed to be ten or twelve feet high at least, but farther north it appeared much higher." Worse yet, the ice appeared to be advancing south, threatening to close the narrow channel entirely. A more prudent captain would have fled at the advance of this wall of ice, but Cook ran along it, taking such risks that he was obliged to slow the *Resolution* to allow the

Discovery to catch up. A wind continually blew from the north, threatening to pile both ships up on the shoals off the land to the south. In the midst of this dangerous situation, Cook ordered his boats into the water to bring aboard some of the walruses that lived on the ice.

Why did he risk it? Because he was conscious of the need of' his crews for fresh meat. Cook wrote, "There were few on board who did not prefer it to salt meat. The fat at first is as sweet as marrow . . . the lean is coarse, black, and rather a strong taste. The heart is nearly as well tasted as that of a bullock."

Midshipman Trevenen added his own thoughts when he later read Cook's words in the printed journal:

Captain Cook here speaks entirely from his own taste which was surely the coarsest that ever mortal was endowed with. It is true that almost everyone ate the flesh at first, but that was only because they were rapaciously hungry, having been fed on nought but salt meat for several months . . . [We continued to eat it] only because he would let us have nothing else to eat. . . . At the same time I [agree] that the sea horses were more wholesome food . . . for which reason Capt. Cook was right in taking every step to prevail on his crew to eat it.

Fog descended on the ships and Cook navigated by the sound of the roaring of the walruses on the encroaching ice pack. The fog cleared to reveal flocks of birds flying south, a sign that summer was waning. Cook accepted defeat once more, and turned back. Already his thoughts were "directed toward finding out some place where we could [take on] wood and water, and in . . . how I should spend the winter, so as to make some improvement to geography and navigation and at the same time be in a condition to return . . . in further search of a passage the ensuing summer."

Trevenen again added a postscript about Cook.

If he failed in, or could no longer pursue, his first great object, he immediately began to consider how he might be more useful in prosecuting some inferior one. Procrastination and irresolution he was a stranger to. Action was life to him and repose a sort of death.

Not so his crews on this voyage, who greeted the decision to turn back with "general joy," according to King. Yet Cook determined to return; he blamed this year's failure on his delaying too long in advancing up the coast. Next year he would be here sooner. If death had not overtaken him first, one wonders how many years Cook would have returned in the search for the impossible.

Even now the ships only narrowly escaped being frozen in the oncoming ice pack. When they finally emerged, Cook sailed back above the Bering Strait to the northern coast of the Chukchi Peninsula, and soon recognized that it was not "the east point of the island of Alaschka, but it is no other than the eastern promontory of Asia."

Some of Bering's observations had proved to be correct; Cook still sought to find something useful in the Russian charts that he carried. Stählin had reported that many of the islands on his map were covered with wood. Cook searched for islands, found none, but after passing south through the Bering Strait, made his way to Norton Sound, the large indentation on the Alaskan coastline, where the shores held wood in abundance.

Anchoring there on September 10, the ship was soon visited by a man paddling one of the single-occupant skin-covered canoes that the Eskimos called *kayaks*. Cook gave him some presents and made signs that the crew wanted food. The man soon returned with two dried salmon. Speaking in a language in which none of the words were intelligible except for the word "captain," the man presented them to Cook.

Cook wrote, "In this we were probably mistaken, because I do not see how he could know that I was the captain." One remembers the young New Zealander on Cook's first voyage who recognized that "a noble man is not lost in a crowd."

Cook now made a fateful decision. He considered heading southeast for the known Russian port of Kamchatka, where he could find safe harbor for the winter. But he doubted that he would be able to refit the ships there and supply them for a major exploration of the coast north of Bering Strait the following summer. In addition, the ships would be frozen into the port for the long winter, and "the great dislike I had to lay inactive for six or seven months" decided him to return to the Sandwich Islands, Hawaii.

Sailing straight south through the Bering Sea—there being no need now to follow the coastline—the ships reached Samgoonoodha Bay on the third of October. On his earlier stop here, an Eskimo had brought Cook a note in Russian, which no one aboard could read. Now the Eskimos brought a surprising present for both Cook and Clerke—a rye loaf with salmon baked inside, along with another note in Russian.

Cook sent a party ashore to find the Russians and "make them understand that we were English, friends, and allies." The party returned with three Russian fur-traders. Soon a fourth Russian appeared, a man named Ismyloff, who claimed to be the commander of the Russians "in this and the neighboring islands." He shared with Cook his own map, showing many of the islands in the Aleutian chain. The Russians told Cook that the prices for food and other supplies at Kamchatka would be very high, strengthening his resolve to spend the winter in Hawaii or neighboring islands.

Violent snowstorms hindered the ships' passage through the

tricky Aleutian straits, and both ships suffered damage to the sails, but they soon encountered a brisk trade wind that took them south.

V

DAWN ON NOVEMBER 26 brought sight of the island of Maui. Cook knew he might have to spend a considerable time in the Sandwich Islands and he wanted to avoid difficulties with the people. He ordered that no one aboard would be allowed to trade with the islanders unless authorized by him or Clerke. Cook had also noted signs of venereal disease among his crews, and he wanted to keep them from contact with the island women.

On November 30 several canoes drew near, bringing an old man named Terreeoboo. Though he was in fact the ruler of Hawaii, the neighboring island to the south, Terreeoboo did not present an imposing figure. King described him as wearing "a very beautiful cap of yellow and black feathers, and a feathered cloak . . . although not an old man, yet he was exceedingly debilitated, and every part of him shook prodigiously . . . at this time his whole body almost was encrusted and the skin peeled off in scabs; his eyes were red and sore." The chief made Cook a present of some small pigs and invited him to bring his ships to an anchorage on Hawaii. Cook agreed.

As he approached the island, Cook was surprised to see the summits of the mountains covered with snow. They were not particularly high, but the snow had the appearance of having been there for ages. Canoes appeared at the approach of the ships, throwing out white streamers as emblems of peace. The islanders paddled around the ships, too shy to respond to

Cook's gestures from the deck to come aboard, but before long trade in pigs, fruit, and edible roots began.

Cook now faced a serious problem with his crews. Understandably exhausted after the long trip through the ice, the crews wanted to go ashore, but Cook would not let them. Furthermore, Cook proposed that the crew give up their daily ration of rum, or grog. The daily ration of grog was a tradition in the British navy until 1970, and Cook's men thought it as important as a daily ration of food.

But Cook wanted to save the remaining supply for the cold weather the ships would face on their next trip to the Arctic. He proposed as a substitute "beer" that could be made from sugar cane obtained from the islanders. He began to serve it as normal rations at the officers' table, and ordered the supply of grog locked up.

The crew, according to John Watts, a midshipman, wrote Cook a letter, protesting both the beer and "the scanty allowance of provisions served them, which they thought might be increased where there was such plenty and that bought for mere trifles."

Cook gathered all hands on deck, wrote Watts, and told them that it was the first time he had heard any complaint about the shortness of the food allowance, and that it would be rectified. Cook added that he understood that they would not drink the beer because they imagined it harmful to their health. He pointed out that they could, and did, eat the sugar cane from which the beer was made. Cook said that he could not help it if they did not choose to drink the beer. "They would be the sufferers as they should have grog every other day provided they drank the sugar cane, but if not the [grog] cask should be struck down into the hold, and they might content themselves with water."

Stubbornly, the crew chose water, and one man expressed his feelings even more vividly by throwing overboard the cask of sugar cane beer on the following night. Cook punished him with twelve lashes, and told the crew, wrote Watts, that "he looked upon their letter as a very mutinous proceeding and that in future they might not expect the least indulgence from him."

Cook may not have admitted it to himself, and no mention of it appears in his journal, but he too was tired. He had not had sufficient rest in England from his previous voyage, and he had met with little but failure on this one. Cook was unused to failure, and he was unaccustomed to "mutinous" behavior in his crews. Hadn't he kept them free from disease by insisting on cleanliness and fresh food? No captain before him had ever had such a record of safety on three long voyages.

To add to Cook's frustration, there was renewed evidence of the careless refitting at Deptford. A rope holding the main topsail gave way in a storm, resulting in the destruction of three of the ship's sails. Cook wrote a long journal entry, uncharacteristically bitter for him, condemning the work done at Deptford, as well as the quality of the rope and canvas issued by the navy. This passage was deleted from the journal before publication by Palliser, who was seeking to preserve his own reputation as comptroller of the navy, in charge of the proper fitting out of naval vessels.

Little happened in the next few weeks. Cook seemed to be sailing aimlessly around the large island. Trade with the Hawaiians continued, giving rise to Cook's comment that they were the most trusting people he had ever met with. No instance of attempted theft had been reported. There was no mention of the traditional shipboard Christmas celebration— without grog it must have seemed bleak.

On January 16, 1779, the ships came to a promising-looking bay. A tumultuous reception began. In Cook's words, "Canoes now began to come off [the island] from all parts, so that before 10 o'clock there were not less than a thousand about the two ships, the most of them filled with people, hogs, and other productions of the island. Not a man brought with him a weapon of any sort."

Bligh, returning from shore in a boat, reported that the harbor offered good anchorage and fresh water, and Cook stopped at last, in the bay called Kealakekua by its inhabitants. Islanders continued to swarm about the ships the following day, so many of them coming aboard that a subchief of Terreeoboo's named Parea finally drove all the visitors from the ships except for a few important people. Parea introduced himself to Cook and wrapped a piece of red cloth around the captain. Having received this tribute—whether as god or great chief—Cook went ashore.

With his simple statement of departure, Cook's journal ends. He was to live a month longer, but the rest of his story is told from the journals of King and Clerke.

King estimated that the reception for Cook included ten thousand people, standing on the beach, on canoes in the harbor, or swimming in the bay. Their voices were raised in song and those ashore began jumping as Cook's boat touched the land. Three or four priests stepped forward to greet Cook. They carried wands tipped with dog's hair and kept repeating a sentence, of which the English could discern nothing but the word *Lono*.

The priests led Cook and his party to a huge structure made of stones. It was about 8 feet high and measured 160 by 60 feet at ground level. The top was flat, with a fence around it on which were stuck human skulls. Nearby was a semicircle of carved images where fruit and hogs had been left as sacrifices.

Led by a priest named Koa, Cook entered the semicircle, followed by ten men bringing a hog and a piece of red cloth. They prostrated themselves on the ground and Koa wrapped the cloth around Cook and presented him with the hog. The priest led Cook to each of the images in the group and made signs indicating he should kiss them. Now another procession of natives arrived, bearing more gifts for Cook, and chanting over and over the name *Lono*.

Modern anthropologists confirm that the welcome was a ceremony acknowledging Cook as an incarnation of the Hawaiians' god Lono. It seems strange that this was not apparent to King, or presumably to Cook, but they were struggling to understand a completely foreign culture, and his experiences in other places kept Cook from jumping to conclusions about islander behavior.

Nonetheless, King was uneasy. After returning to the ship, he wrote, "We [were] very well satisfied with the behavior of our guides, but instead of the very abject and slavish manner . . . we should have been better pleased with the shouts with which our Friendly Islanders [Tongans] received us."

There were some advantages in Cook's new status. When observatories and tents were set up ashore for the men who were sent to gather water and other supplies, the priest tabooed the area so the English would not be bothered. King noted that "The natives sat upon the walls marking our boundary, and none offered to . . . come within the tabooed space without permission."

Cook had more trouble with his own men. Almost daily he ordered a dozen lashes for the men who approached the Hawaiian women; he was still trying to keep the venereal disease from spreading to the island. Moreover, King observed, the men were in great need of rest but Cook's strained relations with the crews kept him from allowing them the usual freedom to go ashore.

In spite of the warm reception, Cook was worried that the continuing presence of his men would deplete the food supply of the area. King conjectured that Cook planned to return to sea at an early date, something that would no doubt cause more resentment among the crew.

On January 26, Terreeoboo arrived at the bay with Koa and a great number of other chiefs. They drew near the ships in canoes. Lieutenant King described their approach:

> Their appearance was very grand, the chiefs standing up [in the canoes] dressed in their cloaks and caps and in the center canoe were the busts of what we supposed were their gods, made of basket work, variously covered with red, black, white, and yellow feathers, the eyes represented by a bit of pearl oyster shell with a black button, and the teeth were those of dogs. The mouths of all were strangely distorted.

At Terreeoboo's invitation, Cook came ashore again. There were no canoes to be seen in the usually busy bay, and the islanders came out of their houses and prostrated themselves on the ground throughout the ceremony that followed. Terreeoboo gave Cook his own cloak, a long garment made entirely of feathers. The chief also put his feathered cap on Cook's head and laid down before him "five or six cloaks more, all very beautiful, and to them of the greatest value," according to Lieutenant King. Cook and Terreeoboo exchanged names, here as elsewhere in the Pacific a sign of friendship and respect. Cook brought the chiefs aboard the *Resolution* and gave them presents in return.

On the 1st of February, one of Cook's most loyal men, William Watman, died. He had been on the previous voyage, and had been a marine for twenty-one years. One of the oldest men aboard ship, his experience at instructing younger men and his loyalty to Cook had been factors in smoothing the relations between captain and crew. Terreeoboo, hearing of Watman's death, asked that he be buried ashore, a request that Cook granted. The Hawaiians interred him at their burial ground in a ceremony that lasted for three days.

Despite the adulation, King sensed a growing eagerness among the islanders to know when the English planned to leave. Cook felt it too, and ordered the camp ashore taken down. On February 4 the ships sailed out of Kealakekua Bay, accompanied by a great number of canoes, which followed them throughout that day and the next.

A sudden squall struck, threatening to overturn the canoes, and Cook allowed the islanders to tie their craft to the ships and come aboard for safety. King noted that many of the island people became seasick. Even so, he wrote, "They do not appear to have the smallest fears as to their own safety with us."

The squalls continued, and on February 8, Cook observed that the rigging on the foretopmast was slack. An inspection showed that the head of the foremast was badly sprung, or split; to make matters worse, the *Resolution*'s unreliable hull had again begun to leak.

There was no other recourse but to return to Kealakekua Bay to repair the damage. "All hands," reports King, were "much chagrined and damning the foremast." It is a strange comment, in view of the reception the ships had received at Kealakekua, and indicates that there was more than one aboard who felt that the reception had been too unusual.

What Cook thought will always remain a mystery, but his officers and men may have realized better than he that Cook's grip on command, so sure and so right in many other places, had slipped. Even Cook could not deal adequately with the requirements of a man thought to be a god.

The squalls continued as the ships again moored at Kealakekua on February 11. By the thirteenth the foremast had been removed and sent ashore with the carpenters and sailmakers. To the Hawaiians, all this activity left a clear message: The

English had returned for an indefinite stay, although Cook had confided to Lieutenant King his intention to make repairs quickly and sail as soon as possible.

The changed attitude of the islanders was quickly perceived. King noticed that very few of the Hawaiians came to greet the men ashore. Terreeoboo was gone, and in his absence it was taboo for canoes to venture into the bay. "This," King wrote, "in some measure hurt our vanity, as we expected them to flock about us, and to be rejoiced at our return."

Unexpectedly, one of the islanders attempted to steal a pair of armorer's tongs. There had been almost no stealing on the previous stay, and, perhaps with the intention of preventing a recurrence, Cook ordered an unusually harsh punishment for the culprit—forty lashes, twice the number that was permitted by naval law to be inflicted on a crew member. After the flogging, the islander was tied to the mainsail.

If the punishment was intended to deter future problems, it failed. On the afternoon of the same day, Cook's men assigned to bring water from a well informed Lieutenant King that "a chief had hindered the natives who he had paid from assisting [them], and that . . . the others were very troublesome."

King, in charge of the parties ashore, assigned a marine to accompany the party to the well. They again returned and said that the islanders were now armed with stones, "and were still more insolent." King accompanied another watering party and with difficulty persuaded the islanders to lay down their stones.

When Cook came ashore, King reported the squabble to him. Cook "gave orders to me that on the first appearance of throwing stones or behaving insolently, to fire ball at the offenders." King passed on the order to the marines.

Even so, more trouble quickly followed. Cook and King heard firing of muskets from the ships in the harbor. When they returned to the beach, they saw that the firing was directed at a canoe paddling swiftly away from the *Discovery*. One of the *Discovery*'s boats was lowered and began to follow. Cook ordered King and two marines to run along the shore and meet the canoe when it landed. By now, however, a crowd of islanders appeared on the shore and hindered King and the marines. The boat landed and its occupants fled inland. Cook followed with more men. He threatened the islanders with punishment if they did not turn over to him the man who had fled in the canoe. King noted, "Whenever the marine made any motion of [aiming his musket], the crowd would recoil back, but it was observable enough that they began to laugh at our threat."

Eventually Cook and King returned to the shore without catching the thief. There they found that the ship's boat that had gone in pursuit had landed and engaged some islanders in a brief fight, in which the islanders beat the sailors soundly and broke all but one of the boat's oars. Though the stolen object, again the armorer's tongs, had been recovered, Cook seethed with anger at the treatment of his men.

The following morning Captain Clerke came to the *Resolution* between six and seven o'clock to inform Cook that one of the *Discovery*'s boats had been stolen during the night. Cook immediately ordered his men to seize all the canoes they could find in the harbor. He sent other men to strategic points to prevent any islanders from escaping by sea.

Clerke returned to the *Discovery*, and Cook went ashore with Molesworth Phillips, the captain of marines, and three boats of armed men. About an hour later, Clerke heard firing on shore. Clerke used his spyglass to try to see what was happening, and

I clearly saw that our people were driven off to their boats but I could not distinguish persons in that confused crowd. The pinnace and launch, however, continued the fire [from their position offshore] and the *Resolu-tion* . . . fired their cannon among [the islanders on the beach.]

Something terrible had happened, and Clerke waited uneasily for news. He went to the *Resolution* to find Molesworth Phillips being treated for spear wounds. Phillips made his report to Clerke:

Cook had landed with the pinnace and launch, leaving the smaller cutter offshore to prevent the escape of any canoes. With Phillips and nine other marines, Cook marched into the village to Terreeoboo's hut. Phillips went inside and found the old king just awakening and apparently unaware of the theft of the boat.

Cook, said Phillips, "proposed to the old gentleman to go on board with him, which he readily agreed to, and we according-ly proceeded toward the boats." Cook obviously planned to take the king hostage, a tactic that had worked in other places, but the Hawaiians reacted differently.

As the English were taking Terreeoboo toward the boats, one of the king's wives came up; weeping and pleading, she begged him not to go. Two other chiefs then "laid hold of him," according to Phillips,

and insisting that he should not, made him sit down; the old man now appeared dejected and frightened. It was at this period we first began to suspect that they were not very well disposed towards us, and the marines . . . hud-dled together in the midst of an immense mob composed of at least two or three thousand people.

Cook's confidence and courage never flagged; facing odds of eleven men against several thousand, he ordered Phillips to draw his men up in a line along the beach. Phillips saw that the islanders were arming themselves with spears and knives. A priest began to chant and made some kind of offering to Cook and Terreeoboo "to divert their attention," according to Phillips.

Cook now gave up the idea of taking Terreeoboo on board, telling Phillips, "We can never think of compelling him to go on board without killing a number of these people." He was about to order his men to enter the boats when a man armed with a long iron spike and a stone came toward him with menacing gestures.

Cook discharged a load of small shot at the man, but it was repelled by the thick matted shield that the man held. Just as Cook had always warned his men, the islanders would become contemptuous of gunfire that had no effect. The other islanders, hearing Cook's shot but seeing that the man he aimed at did not fall, now advanced.

One of the islanders attempted to stab Phillips, who struck him with the butt end of his rifle. Then others in the crowd began to throw stones, and knocked down one of the marines. Cook now fired a second time, with deadly ball that killed one man. Phillips said, "They now made a general attack and the captain gave orders to the marines to fire and afterwards called out 'Take to the boats.'"

Phillips suffered a blow from a stone and then a stab wound. He fired and killed the man who had stabbed him. "The business was now a most miserable scene of confusion," Phillips recalled. "These fellows instead of retiring upon being fired at, as Capt. Cook and I believe most people concluded they would, acted so very contrary a part, that they never gave the soldiers time to reload their pieces." All the English ashore would now have been killed had not the men in the boats opened fire and kept off the islanders until the marines could make their way through the surf to the waiting boats. Phillips saw no more of Cook.

Lieutenant King had been farther up the shore at the English camp when the attack took place. He had a vantage point inferior to Phillips's, but he wrote that the first firing came from the boats, and blamed the massacre on the hot-headed Williamson. King wrote that after the firing from the boats began, Cook turned to signal Williamson to cease fire when the islanders attacked him with his back turned.

The accounts of various eyewitnesses—some of whom were watching the scene through spyglasses from the ships—vary to a great degree. Some blamed Williamson for not coming to Cook's aid. By these accounts, Cook called for the boats to move toward shore to pick up him and the marines, but Williamson stayed off the beach, and by one account threatened to shoot the first man in the boat who pulled a stroke toward shore. Williamson, it must be remembered, was not popular among the officers and men, nor was there any love lost between him and Cook.

It was never certain who gave the fatal wound to Cook. King reported that when "a chief gave him a stab in the neck or shoulder . . . he fell with his face in the water. The Indians set up a great shout and hundreds surrounded the body to dispatch him with daggers and clubs." Besides Cook, four of the marines lost their lives on February 14, 1779.

However it happened, Cook's luck had run out at the age of fifty and his voyages ended. There were many causes, among them his deteriorating relations with the crew; the bad refit of the ships, which caused Cook to return to Kealakekua; the strain on his judgment caused by too many years at sea; and the unpredictable conduct of the islanders. Fancifully, it might be said that having achieved at the end the status of a god, Cook was claimed by the gods themselves—there was nothing more for him to discover on earth.

In the night following Cook's death, the men aboard the *Resolution* and *Discovery* could see the lights of many fires on shore and in the hills. Trevenen wrote, "By the light of the fire, we could plainly perceive the Indians in motion about them, and this sight joined to the awful solemnity and stillness of the night now and then interrupted by their horrid cries and yellings was finely calculated to make an impression on our already agitated feelings."

It was left to Clerke to take command. Clerke had known for some time that he was dying of tuberculosis, and the death of Cook stunned him as much as any man on board, yet he responded as he felt Cook would have.

Many urged Clerke to take revenge. The ships' cannon could destroy the villages along the beach. Clerke realized it was not the way Cook would have chosen. The islanders themselves, after a few days, seemed chagrined by what had happened. They returned what was left of Cook's body after some kind of rites in which it was burned and dismembered. Left untouched were the hands, which were easily recognized by the scar from the accident that Cook had suffered in Newfoundland fifteen years before. Some of the bones were kept by the Hawaiians and carried in an annual religious ceremony, according to a missionary who visited the islands in 1819. Despite his apparent lapse into mortality, the islanders continued to venerate their god Lono who had come to them in the strange form of Captain Cook.

Clerke buried the remains at sea and reported that the islanders anxiously asked him if Lono would forgive them if he returned. In 1792 another English visitor met an islander called Pihere who said he had been the man who killed Cook, "and added with tears that he hoped Lono would forgive him—as he had built several *maraes* to his memory and sacrificed a number of hogs annually at each of them."

The sailors were not to be denied their revenge. Clerke allowed trade to resume, realizing that the *Resolution*'s mast still had to be repaired, and supplies gathered from the shore.

Islanders around the watering place pelted the sailors with rocks, and when an officer gave permission for the sailors to burn down the rock-throwers' shelter nearby, the crew ran wild, burning, according to one account, 150 houses and killing half a dozen islanders. The sailors beheaded two men and stuck the skulls on their boats "as trophies of their vile victory," an officer wrote, "and would have gone on with this shocking piece of barbarity had not they been stopped by the officer on shore." With the help of his officers, Clerke restored peace.

Clerke took command of the *Resolution*, assigning Gore to head the *Discovery*. The ships sailed west over empty ocean, though Clerke did not know it was empty and was following the path Cook might have chosen in search of more discoveries. By the end of March they turned north to Kamchatka. The cold extended farther south than anyone expected. The temperature, which had been in the 80s on April 1, fell to below 30°F by April 10. The weather worsened Clerke's failing health, but he was determined to carry out the orders assigned to Cook.

The ships' hulls continued to leak and the sails to give way under the strain of the interminable voyage. By May 1, the ships reached the settlement of Petropavlovsk on the east coast of Kamchatka. King, Gore, and Webber crossed the peninsula on a sledge to visit the Russian governor. The governor agreed to forward Cook's journal and other reports to England. Seven months later, with the *Resolution* and *Discovery* still at sea, the documents reached London, and the nation mourned the loss of its greatest sailor.

Clerke tried valiantly to cap the voyage with the discovery of the Northwest Passage. He led the ships again through the Bering Strait that summer, hoping to find a hole in the ice sheet through which he might take the ships across the top of North America. The passage was not there. On the twenty-seventh of July the ships gave up the search and returned to the Pacific.

On August 15, Clerke turned over command of the *Resolution* to Lieutenant King. A week later, as the ships drew within sight on Kamchatka, the loyal Clerke died. Gore took command of the expedition. There seemed little to do but to try to refit the ships for the voyage home. The *Discovery* had been badly damaged in the second struggle with the ice, and the *Resolution* remained unreliably leaky.

The ships stayed at Petropavlovsk until October 10. Stopping at Macao, on the China coast, Gore sent upriver to the British trading posts at Canton for more supplies. Cook's men learned that Britain was now at war with France, but that the French had exempted Cook's ships from capture. Unknown to them, Benjamin Franklin, acting for the newly convened Congress of the United States of America, then at war with Great Britain, had issued a similar order to the colonial ships. Franklin called Cook's voyage "an undertaking truly laudable in itself . . . whereby the common enjoyments of human life are multiplied and augmented, and science of other kinds increased to the benefit of mankind." He asked the captains of American ships not to consider Cook's ship "an enemy . . . nor obstruct her immediate return to England."

Unobstructed, and considered even by England's enemies a truly international voyage of discovery, the ships continued on their way. Two of the ships' companies, already thinking ahead, deserted at Macao with the thought of going into the lucrative fur trade that all could see awaited voyagers to the northwest coast of America.

The ships reached the Cape of Good Hope on April 12, 1780. Phillips and Williamson were said to have fought a duel here; tempers still ran high over the memory of the circumstances surrounding Cook's death. The duel was not fatal. Williamson eventually was given command of the *Discovery* after the ships reached England. But as a captain in a battle between the English and French in 1797, he so disgraced himself that he was court-martialled and expelled from the navy. Phillips married James Burney's sister Fanny, but the marriage was an unhappy one. Though he eventually reached the rank of lieutenant colonel in the marines, he was captured and held a prisoner during the Napoleonic Wars. He lived to be almost eighty.

Bad winds, and possibly fear of French ships in the channel, caused Gore to avoid the usual route back to the Port of London. He sailed the long way around the north coast of Scotland. Coming south, the ships sailed past the port of Whitby, where thirty-two years before, Cook had begun his career as a too-old seaman on a coal ship. On October 4, 1780, the ships were in the Thames, after a journey of four years, two months, and twenty-two days.

England embraces its naval heroes, and it made Cook nearly as godlike a character as the Hawaiians had. The three great heroes of English naval and military history are today memorialized in New Zealand, where Cook is regarded much as Columbus is in the United States. On either side of the Cook Strait are the modern cities of Wellington and Nelson.

Cook's widow presided over his memory for the remaining years of her long life. Her two remaining sons died in the service of the Royal Navy. Elizabeth Batts Cook died at the age of ninety-three, 56 years after the death of her famous husband. Before she died, she destroyed the private letters he had written her, ensuring that Captain Cook will always remain something of a mystery—one of the legends of the sea. He let us know as much as he wished about his own character when he wrote that he wished to go "not only farther than any other man has been before me, but as far as I think it possible for man to go."

Bibliography

The Journals of Captain James Cook, edited by J. C. Beaglehole, Vols. 1-4, Cambridge: Cambridge University Press, 1967, 1968, 1969.

Anderson, Romola, and R. C. Anderson. *The Sailing Ship: 6000 Years of History*, New York: Benjamin Blom, Inc., 1971.

Beaglehole, J. C., *The Exploration of the Pacific*, 3rd edition, Stanford, CA: Stanford University Press, 1966.

———. *The Life of Captain James Cook*, London: The Hakluyt Society, 1974.

Begg, A. Charles, and Neil C. Begg, *James Cook and New Zealand*, Wellington, New Zealand: A. R. Shearer, Government Printer, 1969.

Berry, Erick, and Herbert Best, *The Polynesian Triangle*, New York: Funk and Wagnalls, 1968.

Dole, Paul W. (compiler, editor, and annotator), *Seventy North to Fifty South, the Story of Captain Cook's Last Voyage*, Englewood Cliffs, NJ: Prentice-Hall, 1969.

Grattan, C. Hartley, *The Southwest Pacific to 1900*, Ann Arbor, MI: University of Michigan Press, 1963.

Maclean, Alistair, *Captain Cook*, Garden City, NY: Doubleday, 1972.

Napier, William, John Gilbert, and Julian Holland, *Pacific Voyages*, Garden City, NY: Doubleday, 1973.

Phillips-Birt, Douglas, *A History of Seamanship*, Garden City, NY: Doubleday, 1971.

Sharp, Andrew, *The Discovery of the Pacific Islands*, Oxford, England, 1962.

Villiers, Alan, *Captain James Cook*, New York: Scribner's, 1967.

Index

Index